Mandatory Community Service
in High School:
The Legal Dimension

Ronald T. Hyman

Disclaimer

The Education Law Association (ELA) is a private, nonadvocacy, and nonprofit association of educators and attorneys. The opinions expressed in this publication are those of the author and do not represent official views of the Association.

Published by
Education Law Association
300 College Park, Dayton, Ohio 45469-2280
(937) 229-3589
ela@udayton.edu
www.educationlaw.org

About the Author

Ronald T. Hyman is a Professor at Rutgers University, The State University of New Jersey where he has taught since 1966. He earned his Ed.D. degree at Columbia University and his J.D. degree from Rutgers-Newark Law School. He is a member of the New Jersey Bar, the New Jersey State Bar Association, the Education Law Association, the Education Law Special Interest Group of the American Educational Research Association, and the American Association of University Professors. He is the author of numerous articles as well as the author, co-author, or editor of more than 20 books in the fields of education (curriculum, teaching, and supervision) and education law. He was the co-author of a pair of companion books on corporal punishment published by the Education Law Association. He also serves as the Executive Director of the New Jersey School Development Council, a member of the Advisory Board of the New Jersey Center for Law Related Education, and Vice-President of the Rutgers New Brunswick chapter of the American Association of University Professors.

Acknowledgments

I take this opportunity to acknowledge and thank the numerous people who have helped me with this book: the many lawyers involved with community service activity and litigation on "both sides of the street," especially Scott Bullock and Phyllis Jaffe, who provided materials and talked with me about court issues; the executive directors of the service organizations who spoke with me and/or sent me material; the directors and staffs at the schools I spoke with and/or visited, especially Phyllis Walsh, Ron Horowitz, John Battaglia, Rick Musser, and Maurice Tenney; my students and colleagues at Rutgers University who discussed community service issues with me; the volunteers and staffs at the service organizations where I have performed my own community service; the anonymous students whose writings I have reproduced; the Rutgers secretaries and librarians who have helped me create this book; my colleagues in the Education Law Association at whose annual conferences I have spoken on the legal dimension of community service; the Rutgers AAUP Council leaders and the Rutgers administrators who negotiated the faculty research study program that allowed me to devote the Spring 1998 semester to writing this book; Clifford Hooker and Elizabeth T. Lugg, the editors, respectively, of *Education Law Reporter* and *Illinois State School Law Reporter* who permitted me to use parts of my previously pieces that appeared in their journals; and my wife, Suzanne, who has been a constant source of support and guidance.

Dedication

To Matti, Jane, and Naomi, sources of love and joy.
May they grow from strength to strength.

"And I hope it will remind every American there can be no opportunity without responsibility. The great English historian Edward Gibbon warned that when the Athenians finally wanted not to give to society but for society to give to them, when the freedom they wished for most was freedom from responsibility, then Athens ceased to be free."

President William Jefferson Clinton
Remarks on signing the National and Community Service Trust Act of 1993
September 21, 1993

Student Reflection

It is required by _____ H.S. to do ____ hours of community service to graduate. Students and some parents find this unnecessary and ridiculous, even giving up their final walk with the graduating class to prove how ridiculous it is....

My journal barely covered my true feelings about the work, so I am writing a paper.

I had the opportunity to do my community work at the _____Hospital Medical Center Emergency Department, and I jumped at the chance when it was offered to me. I was given the option to work a four hour shift, but eventually I went in at 6 a.m. and worked until 2 p.m.....

Volunteering in an emergency medical facility is highly stressful, as is being a paid employee. We work around the clock to ensure the patient is comfortable or to make them as comfortable as possible. I was assigned to stat med runs for patients and specimen delivery daily. The staff made a point to get me involved so I knew what was going on along with the paid staff members. Overall it was a tiring job, but I looked forward to it every day I had the chance to work....

The first day I worked, I wrapped up a DOA 75-year old man in a white sheet. It was a major turning point of my purpose of life. That day, I decided that whatever job or field I got into I would be working with people, people that were alive and functioning....

Out of all the experiences through high school, the most valuable was out of the classroom and in the real world workplace. I'm thankful that _____ H.S. is ridiculous.

High School Senior,
Graduating class of 1998,
from one of the three community
service programs challenged in
court

TABLE OF CONTENTS

Chapter I: Introduction

For years, voluntary community service in one form or another has existed in many high schools. More recently schools have placed greater emphasis on community service and even have gone so far as to make it a requirement for graduation. How did voluntary community service become a mandatory requirement? Maybe voluntary, extracurricular activitives, such as a marching band participating in a hometown Memorial Day parade, evolved, in some schools, into a voluntary activity for which participating students could earn credit. From there, in some school districts voluntary activity became a graduation requirement set down by their respective boards of education to show their belief in the importance of community service.

In the early 1990s, three major lawsuits filed in federal court challenged the requirements set by three separate school districts that students perform some community service before graduating high school. The three resulting cases in chronological order are *Steirer v. Bethlehem Area School District*,[1,2] *Immediato v. Rye Neck School District*,[3,4] and *Herndon v. Chapel Hill-Carrboro City Board of Education*.[5,6] These three law cases[7] together constitute the legal challenge to the movement, that began in the 1970s and blossomed in the 1980s, to incorporate a service component into the school program as one means of reforming and strengthening the curriculum of high schools. The presentation and analysis of these cases form the core of this book.

The three cases, hereinafter called S*teirer I, Steirer II, Immediato I, Immediato II, Herndon I,* and *Herndon II,* caught the attention of the public and the press. Either as a consequence of that attention

---

[1] 789 F. Supp. 1337, 75 Ed. Law Rep. 273 (E.D. Pa. 1992) [hereinafter Steirer I].

[2] 987 F. 2d 989 [81 Ed. Law Rep. [734]] (3rd Cir. 1993), *cert. denied*, 510 U.S. 824, 114 S.Ct 85, 126 L.Ed. 2d 53 (1993) [hereinafter Steirer II].

[3] 873 F. Supp. 846 [108 Ed. Law Rep. [92]] (S.D.N.Y. 1995) [hereinafter Immediato I].

[4] 73 F. 3d 454 [106 Ed. Law Rep. [85]] (2nd Cir. 1996), *cert. denied*, 519 U.S. 813, 117 S.Ct. 60, 136 L.Ed. 2d 22 (1996) [hereinafter Immediato II].

[5] 899 F. Supp. 1443 [104 Ed. Law Rep. [246]] (M.D.N.C. 1995) [hereinafter Herndon I].

[6] 89 F. 3d 174 [110 Ed. Law Rep. [1037]] (4th Cir. 1996), *cert. denied*, 519 U.S. 1111, 117 S.Ct. 949, 136 L.Ed. 2d 837 (1997) [hereinafter Herndon II].

[7] *A prior case, Bobilin v. Board of Education*, State of Hawaii, 403 F. Supp. 1095 (D. Haw. 1995), also dealt with a student's challenge to "school service" in terms of required cafeteria duty. However, this case did not deal with the rationale for community service as one way to improve the high school. See discussion in the section dealing with the claimed violation of the Thirteenth Amendment.

or as a consequence of a widespread renewed interest in parental rights, legislators began to propose federal and state legislation aimed at strengthening the right of parents to direct the upbringing and education of their children. Under such legislation parents would have the right, some proponents believe, to reject mandatory community service.

Advocates of mandatory community service believe that service is as educationally beneficial to students as are required courses in mathematics, science, the language arts of reading and writing, physical education, health, and history. High school mandatory community service differs from the mandatory community service ordered by a court or board of education as discipline for some types of misbehavior[8] in that it seeks not to punish[9] students but to enrich their lives and benefit the community. While there are some similarities between the curriculum-based programs and the punishment-based programs, this book will deal only with curriculum-based community service as a graduation requirement for all students.

In focusing on the legal dimension of community service as a high school graduation requirement, the chapters that follow will present the purposes of community service (Chapter II); the main elements of the three challenged high school programs, the constitutional claims brought by the three sets of plaintiffs in their lawsuits, the courts' opinions in the three lawsuits (Chapter III); commentary on the three court cases (Chapter IV); proposed and new legislation related to community service programs (Chapter V); the outcomes of community service as found in the court opinions, survey data, and student self-reflections (Chapter VI); and

---

[8] In a recent administrative law decision in New Jersey, the Commissioner of Education upheld a local board of education decision to assign a student to sixty-six hours of community service as partial punishment for his involvement in a bomb scare. *See L. F. and S. F. on Behalf of Their Minor Child, M.F. v. Board of Education of Bridgewater-Raritan Regional School District*, 96 N.J. Adm. Reports 2d (Edu) 897 (1996).

[9] Interview with and proposals by K.G. Popovich, Community Service Suspension Program (1998). Popovich is the vice principal of Old Bridge High School, West Campus. For two newspaper articles on this program published on the day the proposal was approved, but before the official approval, see L. Johnson, "Punishment Will be Work," *Home News Tribune*, March 17, 1998, at 1 and "Community Service Plan for Suspended Students," *The New York Times*, March 17, 1998, at B6. For a longer, more detailed article on the day after the approval see T. Haydon, "Suspended Kids Can Opt to Aid Their Community," *The Star-Ledger*, March 18, 1998, at 15. According to a policy analyst at the Education Commission of the States cited in the article in *The N.Y. Times, supra*, there are "only a handful of [programs] nationwide to put suspended students to work."

the remaining issues not dealt with in the three lawsuits, such as supervision of students and liability for injuries, the need for risk management, standards of good practice of community service, and integrating community service with academic content (Chapter VII).

This book focuses on all three court cases and the related legislation but still provides a substantial look at the rationale, functioning, and outcomes of high school community service programs for readers unfamiliar with the large and growing literature in the education field on the topic of community service. This book, however, does not present community service as a closed historical topic since the legal scene is under constant change.

This book aims to inform the reader about the significant legal aspects of community service, to analyze the court opinions and the related recent legislation, and to point out some possible future changes in the law related to community service. The purpose is also to present briefly the rationale for community service by students as well as the outcomes of implementing service programs. In his remarks on service to announce his forthcoming initiative for the National and Community Service Trust Act of 1993, President Clinton reminded Americans that:

> The concept of community and the idea of service are as old as our history. They began the moment America was literally invented. Thomas Jefferson wrote in the Declaration of Independence, "With a firm reliance on the protection of Divine Providence, we mutually pledge to each other our lives, our fortune, and our sacred honor."[10]

This book is an invitation to the reader to think about community service by high school students as part of the students' education and initiation into our democratic society. This book asks the reader to be prepared for future discussions about community service, parental rights, and student rights by understanding the legal and educational dimensions of community service that have surfaced recently.

---

[10] William Jefferson Clinton, "Remarks on National Service at Rutgers University, New Brunswick, N.J., March 1, 1993," Public Papers of the Presidents of the United States, 1993, 225.

Chapter II: Purposes of Community Service Programs

This chapter will describe community service programs in general and in particular the three programs challenged in the lawsuits discussed in the following ch apters. However, before doing so it is appropriate to deal with a distinction present in the educational literature but not in the lawsuits, a fine but not universally accepted or used distinction made by educators deeply involved in this area of the curriculum.

Defining The Terms Community Service And Service-Learning

Many educators distinguish between the terms community service and service-learning. Community service refers to work or activity performed by students in a not-for-profit civic organization, or in a governmental agency, or directly with people in need of help. This service is in addition to a student's participation in the regular school curriculum. While community service might include one student, during a free period or study hall, tutoring other students in the school during the regular school day, community service typically is an after-school, out-of-school activity. As such, the school's community service program is not integrated into the student's academic curriculum. In addition, community service is much of the time a solo activity.

The term service-learning refers to activity that focuses on experiential learning via service to the community and includes teacher-guided or structured time for reflection. Since many service-learning activities involve groups of students performing their service together, the activity can be tied to a class lesson or project.

Following is a definition of service-learning:

"Service-learning is a method by which young people learn and develop through active participation in thoughtfully-organized service experiences
- That meet actual community needs.
- That are coordinated in collaboration with the school and community.
- That are integrated into each young person's academic curriculum.

• That provide structured time for a young person to think, talk, and write about what the student did and saw during the actual service activity.
• That provide very young people with opportunities to use newly acquired academic skills and knowledge in real life situations in their own communities.
• That enhance what is taught in the school by extending student learning beyond the classroom.
• That help to foster the development of a sense of caring for others."[11]

Despite the fact that many community service programs (including the three programs challenged in court) do not have their service programs integrated with the ongoing academic curriculum and do not have the concomitant teacher-led debriefing sessions, community service programs state the same purposes as service-learning programs and claim the same results. Furthermore, some of the educators, judges, lawyers, legislators, journalists, and parents dealing with community service do not maintain a fine distinction between the two types of program as defined above by advocates of service-learning. These people use the term community service in its broad sense to mean service activity to help the community. This broad sense of the term, therefore, includes both types identified above. That is to say, service activity in this broad sense is the core of the programs that are integrated with the academic curriculum as well as with those programs that are not integated.[12] In this book I shall use the term community service in its broad sense to refer to service activity approved by a high school. Such usuage I believe will accord with the language of the courts.

---

[11] Alliance for Service-Learning in Education Reform, Standards for School-Based Service-Learning 1, (May 1993).

[12] In Maryland, the only state with a statewide requirement for community service, the enacted law uses the term student service, not community service or service-learning. However, the Maryland Student Service Alliance, a public/private partnership within the Maryland State Department of Education, uses the term service-learning to emphasize the "experiential learning" aspect of community service. Title 13A.03.02.03 of the Code of Maryland Regulations, as passed by the State Board of Education in 1992, states: "Student Service. Students shall complete one of the following: (1) 75 hours of student service that includes preparation, action, and reflection components and that, at the discretion of the local school system, may begin during the middle grades; or (2) a locally designed program in student service that has been approved by the State Superintendent of Schools."

Four Purposes Of Community Service

The overall, general purpose of community service is to help prepare students to take their places as responsible citizens in a democratic society. The schools' objectives for community service center on the social, psychological, and intellectual (academic) development of each student so as to lead to the students' successful participation in our democratic society. Whether the underpinning political theory of civic education is one of liberalism (focusing on individual rights and government by consent of the governed) or participatory republicanism (focusing on public virtue and the primacy of civic life and active citizenship), the purpose of civic education is achieved by developing the social, psychological, and intellectual development of students.[13] Civic education is a central role of the school, the sole public institution society has for the preparation of students for their present and future lives as citizens. In a manner of speaking, all education in public schools is, therefore, civic education.[14]

The Supreme Court has pointed out the centrality of education, and civic education in particular, to our society. In 1954 in *Brown v. Board of Education of Topeka*, dealing with school segregation, the court declared:

"Today, education is perhaps the most important function of state and local governments. Compulsory school attendance laws and the great expenditures for education both demonstrate our recognition of the importance of education to our democratic society. It is required in the performance of our most basic public responsibilities, even service in the armed forces.[15] It is the very foundation of good citizenship."[16]

In *Bethel School District No. 403 V. Fraser*,[17] the Supreme Court set the context for examining the free speech claim of the student by first stating the purpose of public education. A critical para-

---

[13] See the review of these two underpinning perspectives of political theory in R. Wade, COMMUNITY SERVICE-LEARNING 4-15 (1997).

[14] For a look at two "orientations" toward community service that are "by no means neatly distinct from one another" see J. Kahne and J. Westheimer, "In the Service of What? The Politics of Service Learning," 77 Phi Delta Kappan 593 (May 1996).

[15] In the context of this discussion linking the Brown decision to community service, it is noteworthy that participation in the military is called service rather than labor, work, time, or something else.

[16] 347 U.S. 483, 493, 74 S.Ct. 686, 691, 98 L.Ed. 873, 880 (1954).

[17] 478 U.S. 675, 106 S.Ct. 3159, 92 L.Ed.2d 549 (1986).

graph in the Court's decision stated the foundational purpose of civic education:

> The role and purpose of the American public school sys-
> tem was well described by two historians, saying "public
> education must prepare pupils for citizenship in the Re-
> public.... It must inculcate the habits and manners of civility
> as values in themselves conducive to happiness and as
> indispensable to the practice of self-government in the
> community and the nation." C. Beard & M. Beard, New
> Basic History of the United States 228 (1968). In *Ambach v.
> Norwick*, 441 U.S. 68, 76-77, 99 S.Ct. 1589, 1594, 60 L.Ed.2d
> 49 (1979), we echoed the essence of this statement of the
> objectives of public education as the "inculcat[ion of] fun-
> damental values necessary to the maintenance of a
> democratic political system."[18]

A review of the educational and legal literature that focuses on community service shows that four main purposes justify community service within the public school required curriculum. The purposes, or objectives, provide coherence and direction to a school's program and to the myriad of details that flow from requiring students to perform community service. Mandatory community service explicitly involves a grounding in values and leads to the teaching of values, a situation that always evokes robust controversy among taxpayers.

First Purpose: The Psychological and Social Development of Students

The first and most commonly cited purpose centers on the psychological and social development benefits students are likely to receive from participating in a community service program. Schools emphasize that students gain a sense of worth, pride, con-fidence, competence, self-awareness, usefulness, and self-esteem as they work with other people in the community.[19] The psycho-logical aspect "aids the transition from the dependency of childhood to the status of adult, able to care for others, to make decisions on one's own, and to feel a sense of competence func-

---

[18] *Id.* at 681.

[19] Steirer II, *supra* note 2, 987 F.2d at 991 and Herndon I, *supra* note 5, 899 F.Supp. at 1452-1453.

tioning in the adult world."[20] The social aspect leads to a "reflective sense of responsibility to the society at large, empathy for the conditions of others, bonding to and participation in social institutions."[21] The courts accepted this type of justification from the three challenged school districts.

Second Purpose: Intellectual and Academic Benefits to Students

There are intellectual or academic benefits that students are likely to gain from participating in community service programs. For example, reflection via discussing, reading, writing, and other means of expression under the guidance of teachers to probe the meaning of the service activity leads students to knowledge and understanding of the structure and problems of a democratic community. Students learn substantive content in science, social studies, and other academic areas as teachers and students relate the service projects to the content under study. In serving and reflecting on their service students develop such skills as problem solving, communicating, public speaking, and developing action plans.[22] Although the three challenged school districts did not emphasize this type of justification, it was present in their submitted briefs, and the courts did accept it in that the material before them included acknowledgement of and reference to its specific points.

Third Purpose: Civic Education

This justification focuses on the benefits that the students gain from the development of social responsibility. Democracy cannot survive without the active participation of citizens in their community's life. Service to the community is an obligation[23] that everyone has — to contribute, not only to take. Obligatory ser-

---

[20] Fred M. Newmann and Robert R. Rutter, The Effects of High School Community Service Programs on Students' Social Development 1-2 (Dec.1983). Final Report. Wisconsin Center for Education Research. ERIC# ED-240-043.

[21] *Id.*

[22] Material distributed by the Maryland State Department of Education; Immediato I, *supra* note 3, 873 F.Supp. at 853; and Boyte, "Community Service and Civic Education," 72 Phi Delta Kappan 765, 766-767 (June 1991).

[23] In the context of this discussion of community service it is worthwhile to note that participation on a jury is called duty, not labor, work, time, or something else. A fundamental aspect of democracy is a people's court and participation in it by every citizen is a duty. Note also that a juror serves on a jury, not works on it.

vice is the price people pay for a democratic life. Community service teaches students the value of community life as well as teaching them their responsibilities to the community that has nurtured them. Community service while in school, therefore, fosters a sense of community in young citizens and leads to the survival of the democratic community.[24] The courts accepted this purpose, too.

Fourth Purpose: The Community Benefits

This purpose focuses on the benefits afforded to the community at large and thereby on the goodwill established between the school and the community. Such goodwill benefits the students indirectly. This goodwill purpose is related to, but not the same as, the civic education/democracy purposee. The gain with this fourth purpose is a concrete one in terms of economics and community relations. Civic organizations gain from the work of the students and from the money saved by having free labor from the students. The schools gain from the goodwill established with the adults who recognize that the students are helping the community by increasing their participation in and responsibility for community life and by partially paying back the costs of their free schooling. This goodwill leads to acceptance of the schools' costs to the community.

Part of this fourth justification stems from the role played by community service programs in changing their high schools and their communities.[25] On the one hand, community service programs arise when schools begin to reform their curriculums and activities to meet changing needs. On the other hand, community programs arise not out of curricular reforms but as the spur to curricular reforms. Educators and community leaders who seek to energize and revitalize a high school may use a community service program as the catalyst for school reform, knowing that concerned and involved students, parents, teachers, and community leaders will create a climate that incubates further reform. While community service is at times a result of school reform, it is at other times the leader of or instrument for school reform. It is a

---

[24] For example, see Steirer I, *supra* note 1, 789 F.Supp. at 1339.
[25] For an analysis of service learning as reform that is "bubbling up rather than trickling down" see J. Nathan and J. Kielsmeier, "THE SLEEPING GIANT OF REFORM," 72 Phi Delta Kappan 739 (June 1991). See also other articles in the same issue of that journal, including V. Anderson & others, "COMMUNITY SERVICE LEARNING AND SCHOOL IMPROVEMENT IN SPRINGFIELD, MASSACHUSETTS," at 761.

response to the call for reform as well as the igniter of further reform. In both cases the participating students benefit indirectly
from the overall reform and goodwill created with the community. In this sense community service programs create a win-win
situation for the students, the school, and the community.

The School Districts Under Challenge Define Purpose Behind Mandatory Community Service

The schools that were challenged in court did not categorize
and label the four purposes of their community service programs.
This approach by the defendant schools was, and still is, consistent with what schools usually do. Schools generally list their
specific purposes or give examples of them. To obtain a feeling
for the purposes of community service, as expressed by schools
for their community service programs, it is worth while to read
those purposes as presented to the courts, or reported by the courts,
or published in the education literature. The following statements
of purposes are representative of what the literature claims about
community service:
[T]he purposes of the community service program include the
following:
  a. To help students acquire life skills;
  b. To help students learn about the significance of render-
       ing service to their community;
  c. To give students a sense of worth;
  d. To give students a sense of pride;
  e. To teach students about community organizations
  f. To give students a sense of appreciation of the worth of
       community organizations;
  g. To help students understand their responsibilities as
       citizens in dealing with community issues;
  h. To teach students that their concerns about people
       and events in the community can have positive effects;
  i. To improve students' self-esteem;
  j. To improve the students' ego and moral development;
  k. To give students the opportunity to explore new roles,
       identities and interests;
  l. To enhance the students' willingness to take and
       accept new challenges;

m. To have students assume responsibility and to accept the consequences of their actions;

n. To develop intellectual development and academic learning in such areas as the expression of ideas,reading, and record-keeping;

o. To promote higher-level thinking skills such as open-mindedness;

p. To enhance the skills of learning from experience;

q. To have students learn about and be exposed to service-related skills.[26]

"The Program is aimed at teaching skills and habits perceived by Defendants as essential for good citizenship. The Program, we are told, 'allows students to develop a wide range of personal intellectual, academic and social skills—such as teamwork, problem-solving, negotiation, communication, planning, and evaluation—that will help them become effective employees, colleagues, citizens, and leaders.'"[27]

"Service-learning will help students understand many of the social issues that they learn about in school. It will also help them see their roles as citizens, as active participants in the solution of our most critical problems as a nation. Students involved in service-learning typically demonstrate social, personal, and intellectual growth and development. They increase their teamwork and problem solving skills, as well as leadership and initiative. Their self-respect increases as they see that they can tackle tough problems and succeed."[28]

"[Service-learning] has more to do with becoming a mature adult than any academic exercise; and it is at least the equal of academic effort in building an understanding of others, the capacity to be an effective citizen, and the promise of leading a balanced life in an increasingly complex world."[29]

---

[26] Thomas Dolusio, Superintendent of Schools, Bethlehem (Pa.) Area School District, in his affidavit to the district court, quoted in Steirer I, *supra* note 1, 789 F.Supp. at 1339.

[27] Immediato I, *supra* note 3, 873 F.Supp. at 853, quoting from an affidavit submitted by L. Richard Bradley, an Ohio educator, in an amicus curiae brief submitted as support for the Rye Neck (NY) School District.

[28] Maryland State Department of Education, Service Learning Fact Sheet #4, October 1994.

[29] Harold Howe II, formerly U.S. Commissioner of Education and Vice President of the Ford Foundation for Education and Public Policy, Foreword, to Service Learning: Ninety-sixth Yearbook of the National Society for the Study of Education iv, v (Joan Schine ed., 1997).

"The educational justification for requiring courses that further the development of democratic citizens is a very old one.... When students use experience in the community as a basis for critical reflection and turn that reflection into a tool to examine the nature of democratic communities and the role of the citizen in them, they learn about the nature of liberty, they uncover the interdependence of self and other, and they expose the intimate linkage between rights and responsibilities. Education-based community service programs empower students even as they teach them."[30]

"A service program is rooted in the conviction that schooling at its best concerns itself with the humane application of knowledge to life. Service is concerned with helping others, but, above all, it is concerned with improved learning. It is about helping students to discover the value of the curriculum, and to see that, in the end, formal learning must be considered useful not just economically but socially as well."[31]

In summary, while some educators make a distinction between two terms found in the literature, the judges, lawyers, plaintiffs, and schools involved in the three court cases treated in this book did not do so. In accord with the language of the courts, as well as the language of the general public, the term community service in this book will be an inclusive one, referring to all varieties of community service approved by high schools. Such community service has four main purposes that justify a school board's policy to mandate it or include it on a voluntary basis. These four purposes are psychological and sociological developmental benefits to students; the intellectual or academic benefits to students; the civic education of students in responsibility for the life of their community; and the benefits to the community at large, including the financial benefits and the goodwill established between the school and its community.

---

[30] Benjamin R. Barber, Professor of Political Science and Director of the Walt Whitman Center for the Culture and Politics of Democracy at Rutgers University, in an affidavit submitted, as part of an amicus curiae brief in support of the defendants' motion for summary judgment, to the United States District Court for the Middle District of North Carolina (for Herndon I, *supra* note 5).

[31] Ernest L. Boyer, President of the Carnegie Foundation for the Advancement of Teaching, Foreword to Charles H. Harrison, Student Service ix (1987).

Chapter III: The Three Court Cases

Introduction

A significant spur to the community service initiative came from Ernest L. Boyer, president of the Carnegie Foundation for the Advancement of Teaching. Boyer, in his book *High School: A Report on Secondary Education in America*, reported on his visits to high schools, his review of the literature, his talks with colleagues in and out of education, and his considerations of a variety of alternatives. Boyer concluded, among other things, that "the time has come...to improve instruction and give students more opportunities for service in anticipation of their growing civic and social responsibilities as they become adults."[32] Later in his book he amplified his conclusion, saying:

"We conclude that during high school young people should be given opportunities to reach beyond themselves and feel more responsively engaged. They should be encouraged to participate in the communities of which they are a part. Therefore, we recommend that every high school student complete a service requirement."[33]

During the next ten years many school districts began their investigations and discussions about instituting a service requirement as a condition for graduation. The Bethlehem (Pennsylvania) Area School District began its discussions formally at least as early as March 1989 and finally adopted its service program on April 30, 1990, effective at the beginning of the new school year in September. By September 19, 1990, Lynn Ann Steirer, David Stephen Moralis, and their parents filed suit against the school district, members of the school board, and the superintendent. Thus, the Bethlehem case became the first major case challenging mandatory community service. Similar processes followed in the early 1990s at the Rye Neck High School (located in Mamaroneck, NY, a northern suburb of New York City in Westchester County) and Chapel Hill-Carrboro City High School (North Carolina) where

---

[32] Ernest L. Boyer, High School: A Report on Secondary Education in America, 7 (1983).
[33] *Id*. at 209.

complaints were filed against two similar high school service programs on the same day, April 19, 1994.[34]

Each of the three suits began with two families of parents and students. In *Steirer* both families remained from the beginning to the end. However, in *Immediato* and *Herndon* only one family each remained all the way throughout the proceedings. Private attorneys represented the *Steirer* plaintiffs in the district and appellate courts. The Institute for Justice, a legal organization headquartered in Washington, D.C., which describes itself on the Internet as "a courtroom champion for individual liberty, free market solutions, and limited government,"[35] represented the *Steirer* plaintiffs in their petition for a writ of certiorari[36] to the Supreme Court. The Institute for Justice represented the *Immediato* and *Herndon* plaintiffs from the very beginning to the end of their suits. The school districts all had their own private attorneys represent them through the entire proceedings.

Essential Common Elements of the Challenged Programs

The three programs in the Bethlehem, Rye Neck, and Chapel Hill high schools shared and still share essential elements. The programs stated that their aim is to teach "skills and habits perceived [to be] essential for good citizenship,"[37] to teach the students about their communities, to help students learn life skills, to teach students their responsibilities as citizens, to help "students to develop a wide range of personal, intellectual, academic, and social skills—such as teamwork, problem-solving, negotiation, commu-

---

[34] Facts on these cases were compiled from the published district and appellate court decisions, the various briefs by plaintiffs, defendants, and amici curiae, the joint appendices filed with the courts, the plaintiffs' petitions for certiorari, the defendants' briefs in opposition to the petitions for certiorari, personal interviews with people directly involved with the cases, material distributed by the three school districts, and newspaper articles. (All memorandums, briefs, and articles referenced throughout this monograph are on file with the author.)

[35] <http://www.ij.org> as of Fall 1997.

[36] A petition for a writ of certiorari (sometimes simply petition for certiorari) is the Latin-based term for the formal request to the Supreme Court to hear a case when the Court has discretion to choose the cases it will hear. Sometimes the term used is put completely into English as petition for certification. If certification is granted, the effect is to order the lower court to send the record to the Supreme Court so it can proceed to hear the appeal.

[37] *Immediato I*, 873 F. Supp at 853.

nication, planning, and evaluation,"[38] and to provide experiential opportunities to develop a sense of pride from their work and decision-making.[39]

The Bethlehem, Rye Neck, and Chapel Hill programs require 60, 40, and 50 hours of service, respectively, to be completed anytime during the four years of high school; the programs are mandatory (except for special education students in Bethlehem); and there are no opt-out provisions. Students must work without pay for a private or public nonprofit organization that serves the community, and they may not displace paid employees. Students may choose an organization from pre-approved lists or submit their choices of nonlisted groups for approval. The lists offer many alternatives, ranging from governmental agencies to schools to religious organizations sponsoring nonreligious care for the ill, young, or elderly. Students must submit a record of their community service activities, indicating the type of service performed, the date and number of hours of the service, and some comments about the service. See Figures 1-7 (pages 55-61) for examples.[40]

Variations among the three programs exist in regard to their administration, specific writing requirements, division of hours among types of service, and other particulars. These variations are not critical, however, to the central characteristic of these mandatory programs: high school students are required to perform some unpaid service to their communities in order to receive their graduation diplomas. This requirement is based on the beliefs that a service experience is educative and that community service primarily benefits the students as citizens living in a democratic community.

---

[38] *Id.* and Herndon I, 899 F. Supp at 1452. The same words are found in two cases in that the quotation comes from an affidavit attached to the amicus briefs submitted to both courts by the American Alliance for Rights and Responsibilities in support of the defendant boards of education.

[39] For a list of seventeen purposes offered by the superintendent of the Bethlehem Area School district *see* Steirer I, 789 F. Supp. at 1339.

[40] Figures 1 & 2 are from Community Service Program (April 1990), distributed to all students by the Bethlehem High School; Figures 3 & 4 are from the Rye Neck High School and taken from the Joint Appendix, as submitted for Immediato II to the United States Court of Appeals, Second Circuit; and Figures 5, 6, & 7 are from the Chapel Hill High School and taken from the Joint Appendix, as submitted for Herndon II to the United States Court of Appeals, Fourth Circuit. These forms are significant because the plaintiffs complained that providing the data for the completion of these forms violated the students' rights.

Constitutional Challenges

Before dealing with the constitutional violations claimed by the plaintiffs it is necessary to point out that the plaintiff parents and students did not object to serving their communities per se. In fact, the students stated that they already had performed community service, for example, in assisting with certain Girl Scout activities and certain athletic activities in the junior high school.[41] Nor did the plaintiffs seek to revise their schools' community service programs, for example, by decreasing the number of required hours of service or by changing the nature of the reports students had to file. Nor did the plaintiffs seek to deny their local boards of education the right to set the curriculums of their schools in terms of the knowledge, skills, and values to be taught in the established courses.

Rather, the plaintiffs, essentially, sought:

> ...only to opt out of certain objectionable programs required by the public schools. Public schools would still have vast discretion to determine their curriculum, to experiment, and to teach whatever values they choose, while parents would have the ability to exempt their children from certain programs that require actions that have traditionally been left to family decision-making.[42]

The plaintiffs together raised a series of questions to the courts, claiming violations of the First, Ninth, Thirteenth, and Fourteenth Amendments to the Constitution of the United States. No single, specific claim is common to all three cases when the litigation histories, stretching from the complaints filed in the federal district courts to the petitions to the Supreme Court for writs of certiorari, are considered. Figure 8 (page 62) shows the distribution of the five claimed constitutional violations in terms of specific substan-

---

[41] Steirer I, 789 F. Supp. at 1341.
[42] Immediato's Petition for a Writ of Certiorari at 23, for Immediato I.

tive issues discussed by the judges.[43] It also indicates where the appellate courts disagreed with the reasoning of their respective district courts even though the appellate courts still affirmed the decisions and held unanimously for the defendants. As noted in Figure 8, the Supreme Court denied certiorari for all three sets of plaintiff students and parents.

Because the courts treated the plaintiffs' five constitutional challenges in a similar manner and used almost the same precedents and reasoning to support their holdings, the review below of the three court cases will look at the lawsuits across claims rather than at each case separately. The focus will be on the three appellate court decisions, which at this time are the highest court decisions available on mandatory community service. (No Supreme Court decisions exist because the Court denied certiorari each time without comment.)

Thirteenth Amendment Prohibition of Involuntary Servitude

1. Prior Lawsuits Challenging Mandatory Community Service

The recent lawsuits challenging the constitutionality of mandatory community service as a condition for graduation from high school follow the path of a long and old line of suits seeking relief based on the Thirteenth Amendment's prohibition of involuntary

---

[43] The plaintiffs in Steirer claimed a violation of the Fourteenth Amendment but did not explicate what aspect of that amendment was pertinent. It appears that the plaintiffs invoked the Fourteenth Amendment in their efforts to strengthen their request for due process that would yield a strict scrutiny review of their First Amendment claim. The Steirer courts discussed only the plaintiffs' First Amendment claim. Then they just said that because the First Amendment claim failed there was no need to consider the Fourteenth Amendment issue of whether the state had "a compelling interest in implementing a mandatory community service program. Similarly, in Immediato and Herndon the plaintiffs raised Ninth Amendment claims tied with their Fourteenth Amendment parental liberty claims. The courts discussed the parental liberty claims in terms of the Fourteenth Amendment's substantive due process precedents and held that the claims lacked merit. There is no discussion of Ninth Amendment jurisprudence either by the plaintiffs in their briefs or the judges in their decisions.

servitude. The Thirteenth Amendment, ratified on December 18, 1865, states in its entirety:

> Section 1. Neither slavery nor involuntary servitude, except as a punishment for crime whereof the party shall have been duly convicted, shall exist within the United States, or any place subject to their jurisdiction.
> Section 2. Congress shall have power to enforce this article by appropriate legislation.

The Thirteenth Amendment's prohibition against slavery and involuntary servitude has always barred forced labor "enforced by the use or threatened use of physical or legal coercion," according to Justice O'Connor in the historical survey of Supreme Court precedents in her opinion in *United States v. Kozminski*.[44] Thus, in *Kozminski* the Court affirmed the government's case against the Kozminskis for physically coercing two mentally retarded men to labor on a Chelsea, Michigan, dairy farm "in poor health, in squalid conditions, and in relative isolation from the rest of society."[45] The Kozminski family did not provide the men (both were in their sixties but "viewed the world and responded to authority as would someone 8 to 10 years") with proper nutrition, housing, clothing, and medical care.[46] The men had been working on the Kozminski farm for 10-16 years.

In another case, the Supreme Court decided that peonage, a condition in which a person (a peon) is coerced by a threat of legal action to work off a debt to a master, is barred by the Thirteenth Amendment's prohibition against involuntary servitude.[47] The Supreme Court stated that legislation by Congress "denouncing peonage" is "not limited to the territories or other parts of the strictly national domain, but is operative in the states and wherever the sovereignty of the United States extends."[48]

On the other hand, exceptions exist such that not every example of forced labor has been deemed to constitute involuntary servitude. The Supreme Court has held that the government's requirement of people to perform their "civic duties" is not a violation of the Thirteenth Amendment. Thus, a public-need

---

[44] 487 U.S. 931, 944, 108 S.Ct. 2751, 101 L.Ed. 2d 788 (1988).
[45] *Id.* at 934.
[46] *Id.* at 935.
[47] Clyatt v. United States, 197 U.S. 207, 25 S.Ct. 429, 49 L.Ed. 726 (1905).
[48] *Id.* at 218.

exception to forced labor, based on civic duties deemed to be necessary for a democratic society, has led the Court to uphold:

- **road and bridge work** for every able-bodied man, age 21-45, "for six days of not less than 10 hours each in each year when summoned to do so"; the Supreme Court ruled that such work did not constitute either the involuntary servitude or the slavery prohibited by the Thirteenth Amendment."[49]
- **military service**; The Supreme Court said, "...we are unable to conceive upon what theory the exaction by government from the citizen of the performance of his supreme and noble duty of contributing to the defense of the rights and honor of the nation as a result of the war declared by the great representative body of the people can be said to be the imposition of involuntary servitude, in violation of the prohibition of the 13th Amendment"[50]
- **testimony and jury duty**; the Supreme Court, in ruling that testimony duty did not violate the Fifth Amendment, said that it is "'clearly recognized that the giving of testimony and the attendance upon court or grand jury in order to testify are public duties....The personal sacrifice involved is a part of the necessary contribution of the individual to the welfare of the public. *Blair v. United States*, 250 U.S. 273, 281.' ...There is likewise no substance to the petitioner's argument that the $1-a-day payment is so low as to impose involuntary servitude prohibited by the Thirteenth Amendment."[51]

Other federal courts when faced with claims of involuntary servitude have upheld:

- **"national importance" work for conscientious objectors to war;**[52] the court said that the service work required of the plaintiff-appellant was work of national importance "in lieu of army service which might have been required of appellant, the substitution being allowed as of grace because of conscientious objection to military service."[53]

---

[49] Butler v. Perry, 240 U.S. 328, 60 L.Ed. 672, 674 (1916).
[50] Selective Draft Law Cases, 245 U.S. 366, 390, 165, 62 L.Ed. 349, 35 (1918).
[51] Hurtado v. United States, 410 U.S. 578, 589, 93 S.Ct. 1157, 1164, 35 L.Ed. 2d 508, 518 (1973).
[52] Heflin v. Sanford, 142 F. 2d 798 (5th Cir. 1944).
[53] *Id*. at 800.

- **pro bono legal representation** of clients by attorneys as a condition of practicing law; the court ruled, "Courts have long recognized that attorneys, because of their profession, owe some duty to the court and to the public to serve without compensation when called on."[54]
- **cafeteria duty for students** in grades 4-12 for no more than seven full days in one school year; the district court of Hawaii stated that it was "this Court's firm conclusion, on the basis of the balances struck by the Supreme Court in the past, that the imposition is more than outweighed by the conceded public benefit involved."[55]
- **the government collecting liquidated damages**[56] from a doctor who participated in the National Health Service Corps scholarship program but declined afterwards to perform the required service upon finishing medical school. The court said, "Because the Government has not sought to compel service—and Redovan may choose to have a civil money judgment entered against him in lieu of service—the enforcement of the government's rights in this lawsuit does not constitute peonage or some other form of involuntary servitude."[57]
- **offering to prisoners an option** of participating in a work-release program, even though the consequence of not working and thereby staying in jail may be painful; the court stated, "The choice of whether to work outside of the jail for 20 dollars a day or remain inside the jail and earn nothing may have been 'painful' and quite possibly illegal under state law, but the evidence shows that neither Watson nor Thrash was forced to work or continued to work against his will."[58]

---

[54] United States v. 30.64 Acres of Land, 795 F. 2d 796 (9th Cir. 1986) and United States v. Bertoli, 994 F. 2d 1002 (3rd Cir. 1993).

[55] Bobilin v. Board of Education, State of Hawaii, 403 F. Supp. 1095, 1104 (D. Hawaii 1975).

[56] Liquidated damages is the term used for the amount of money a party to an agreement can collect if another party breaks some obligation in the agreement.

[57] United States v. Redovan, 656 F. Supp. 121, 129 (E.D. Pa. 1986), aff'd. 826 F. 2d 1057 (3rd Cir. 1987).

[58] Watson v. Graves, 909 F. 2d 1549, 1552-1553 (5th Cir. 1990).

• **a county's workfare program** whereby the receipt of public assistance was conditioned on the recipient's participation in a county work program;[59] the court said, "State work programs are one valid way of encouraging the recipients of public assistance to return to gainful employment. They do not constitute involuntary servitude...."[60]

In sum, physical and/or legal coercion are two necessary elements of forced labor that constitutes involuntary servitude. However, not all forced labor may be categorized as involuntary servitude because of exceptions made by the courts. The exceptions are based on the degree of work required, the public need for such work, and the alternatives available to the person who is required to work. As we turn now to the specific cases concerning mandatory community service in high school, we shall see these same elements become central to the one claim brought initially by all three sets of plaintiffs in their respective district courts: the plaintiffs claim that mandatory community service as a condition for graduation from high school violates the Thirteenth Amendment prohibition against involuntary servitude.

2. Plaintiffs' Claim of Involuntary Servitude

The plaintiff's presented a "novel" claim and argument based on what they called "the plain meaning" of the Thirteenth Amendment. "Plaintiffs' claim is novel. The issue of whether mandatory community service constitutes involuntary servitude under the Thirteenth Amendment has not been addressed by any decision that the parties or Court have discovered."[61] The plaintiffs' two-prong claim was that as students they (1) were required to work for or provide service to someone else without pay and (2) would

---

[59] Brogan v. San Mateo County, 901 F. 2d 762 (9th Cir. 1990).

[60] *Id.* at 764. *See also* Delgado v. Milwaukee County, 611 F. Supp. 278 (E. D. Wis. 1985).

[61] Steirer I, 789 F.Supp. at 1341. This statement by Judge Huyett is a bit odd in that three pages later he refers to Bobilin v. Board of Education, State of Hawaii, 403 F.Supp. 1095 (D. Hawaii 1975) that also dealt with a claim by a student based on the prohibition of involuntary servitude. Perhaps Judge Huyett understood Bobilin merely to be about a narrow state regulation requiring cafeteria duty and not community service in general. Perhaps the judge did not believe that cafeteria duty constituted a community service program.

not receive diplomas from their public high schools unless they did so. For them the forced labor without pay, along with the legal coercion in the form of not being eligible for diplomas, constituted involuntary servitude. They used *Bailey v. Alabama* for the definition of involuntary servitude, namely, "that control by which the personal service of one man is disposed of or coerced for another's benefit."[62]

The students claimed that a community service program is unlike other programs of their high schools. "The direct provision of service to others is what distinguishes compulsory student service from any other school-required activity. Students are not serving or laboring for others in English or physical education classes."[63] Furthermore, the students felt coerced in that the available alternatives appeared to them not to be viable alternatives. That is to say, they saw the options of going to private school, transferring on a tuition-paying basis to a different public school that did not require community service, hiring home tutors, and continuing in their respective high schools for other credits and then applying for a General Education Development (G.E.D.) certificate as too expensive and too burdensome for their families. For the plaintiffs these options did not offer relief and were unsuitable to the public school setting.

3. The Courts' Response to Plaintiffs' Claim of Involuntary Servitude

The courts rejected the plaintiffs' claim with several common justifications. The courts' rejections varied slightly so as to fit the specific facts of each case, the precise wording used by the plaintiffs in their claims, and the precedents developed in each circuit. The first and primary justification centers on the meaning of the term involuntary servitude. Thus, for the appeals courts the threshold question was: What does the term involuntary servitude mean? With the threshold question answered, the courts then proceeded to answer the legal issue, which was whether mandatory community service as a high school graduation requirement constitutes a violation of the prohibition against involuntary servitude under the Thirteenth Amendment.

---

[62] 219 U.S. 219, 241, 31 S.Ct. 145, 151, 55 L.Ed. 191, 201 (1911).
[63] Herndon's Brief to the United States Court of Appeals for the Fourth Circuit at 34.

For their guidance the courts turned to *Kozminski* as the most recent Supreme Court case dealing with the definition of the term involuntary servitude. There, in the opening paragraph of her decision, Justice O'Connor noted that the Court had to "determine the meaning" of the term.[64] O'Connor went on to say, "The primary purpose of the Amendment was to abolish the institution of African slavery as it had existed in the United States at the time of the Civil War, but the Amendment was not limited to that purpose; the phrase 'involuntary servitude' was extended to 'cover those forms of compulsory labor akin to African slavery which in practical operation would tend to produce like undesirable results.'"[65]

The Court then reviewed other cases, noting two key points that subsequently offered guidance regarding mandatory community service in high school. First, the Court noted that the Thirteenth Amendment "does not prevent State or Federal Governments from compelling their citizens, by threat of criminal sanction, to perform certain civic duties."[66] Second, the precedents of the Court show that involuntary servitude involves "the use or threatened use of physical or legal coercion."[67] In this way, the Court noted some exceptions to the Amendment's prohibition and also set physical and legal coercion as two basic elements in the definition of the term involuntary servitude.[68] After their examination and acceptance of the meaning of involuntary servitude, as offered by Justice O'Connor in *Kozminski*, the lower courts reviewed cases for parallels with community service. They reviewed cases that had been deemed to be involved with involuntary servitude as well as cases that had been deemed as exceptions to the Thirteenth Amendment. The courts concluded that the facts of the high school cases before them did not reach the level of involuntary servitude.

---

[64] Kozminski, 487 U.S. at 934.

[65] *Id.*, quoting Butler, at 240 U.S. at 332 *and also citing* Robertson v. Baldwin, 165 U.S. 275, 282 (1897) *and* Slaughter-House Cases, 16 Wall. 36, 69 (1873).

[66] *Id.* at 944.

[67] *Id.*

[68] The Court also explicitly noted that it had never interpreted involuntary servitude "to prohibit compulsion of labor by other means, such as psychological coercion." But it drew "no conclusions from this historical survey about the potential scope of the Thirteenth Amendment." Kozminski 487 U.S. at 944. Thus, the Court did not take the opportunity to comment on United States v. Mussry, 726 F. 2d 1448 (9th Cir. 1984) which broadened the scope of the prohibition beyond just physical or legal coercion, which might have been relevant to the cases concerning mandatory community service in high school.

Key points of the cases involved a matter of degree, "like in so many thorny legal distinctions."[69] One court said that the number of hours of service required of the students (in the three cases ranging from 40 to 60 over four years of high school) was "not severe."[70] Moreover, the "nature of the work and conditions under which it must be performed are hardly onerous."[71] The threat of not graduating from high school, which admittedly did exist, did not "rise to the level of 'physical or legal coercion,'"[72] as specified in *Kozminski.*

In short, for the *Steirer II* court there was "no basis or logic that would support analogizing a mandatory community service program in a public high school to slavery."[73] All three appellate courts used this line of analysis. The Third Circuit Court of Appeals in adopting this line of reasoning explicitly commented that it was not using the reasoning of its district court.[74] The district court had relied on the point that student community service was a public benefit for saving taxpayers money.

The courts rejected the Thirteenth Amendment involuntary servitude claim also because of the related reason that the students did have alternatives to performing the required community service. Despite the fact that the plaintiffs claimed that they had no way to opt out of community service, one court concluded that the plaintiffs had several options: students could "avoid the program and its penalties by attending private school, transferring to another public high school, or studying at home to achieve a high school equivalency certificate. While these choices may be economically or psychologically painful, choices they are, nonetheless."[75]

The Third Circuit Court emphasized that in the cases where forced labor did not constitute involuntary servitude, there was

---

[69] Immediato II, at 73 F.3d at 459.
[70] *Id.* at 460.
[71] *Id.*
[72] Herndon II, 89 F.3d at181.
[73] Steirer II, 987 F.2d at1000.
[74] The Third Circuit Appellate Court noted that its district court "placed considerable reliance" on Bobilin, and found Bobilin's reasoning "persuasive" in that the Hawaiian schools by saving tax money were serving the public rather than the private interest. The appellate court chose not to depend on that analysis to reject the plaintiffs' Thirteenth Amendment claim and used a Kozminski analysis instead to affirm the district court's decision. Steirer II, 987 F.2d at 998.
[75] Immediato II, 73 F.3d at 460. Note that the court by using the word "painful" alludes to Watson v. Graves, *supra.*

"no compulsion because the individuals had alternatives to performing the labor....The fact that these choices may not be appealing does not make the required labor involuntary servitude."[76] In short, the courts concluded that the plaintiffs had options that may have been unappealing and that might have led the plaintiffs to feel that the community service programs were not voluntary. However, those very choices led the judges to reject the claim of involuntary servitude. Because alternatives existed, involuntary servitude was absent.[77]

Finally, the courts also rejected the involuntary servitude claim because the high school mandatory community service programs promoted educational benefits for the students. The courts examined the records which included affidavits as to the purposes of the programs. One superintendent listed 17 educational purposes for the students' benefit.[78] The Third Circuit concluded that the service programs were "primarily designed for the students' own benefit and education, notwithstanding some incidental benefit to the recipients of the services."[79]

The courts noted that in all programs the students had choices within their program as to what types of service they would perform. Furthermore, the students did not perform exploitive work (for example, students were not required to wash their teachers' cars, or paint their houses, or do other chores of a primitive nature like mopping floors and collecting trash). On the contrary, students could work with people directly, for example, by tutoring elementary students in arithmetic or perform service for people indirectly by working for organizations such as the Red Cross or the county recycling program.

The two *Immediato* courts in particular drew on an analogous case decided in their circuit. In *Jobson v. Henne* mental patients complained that the amount of work and the type of work they were required to perform in a state hospital constituted involuntary servitude.[80] The Second Circuit Court of Appeals held that a

---

[76] Steirer II, 987 F.2d at1000.

[77] The Fourth Circuit Court of Appeals noted that its district court relied on Lee v. Weisman, 505 U.S. 577, 112 S.Ct. 2649, 120 L.Ed. 2d 467 (1992). (First Amendment Establishment Clause claim against high school graduation prayer). The appellate court concluded that the district court's "reasoning was flawed and its reliance on Weisman was "misplaced regarding voluntariness."

[78] Steirer I, 789 F.Supp. at1339.

[79] Steirer II, at 987 F.2d at 1000.

[80] 355 F. 2d 129 (2nd Cir. 1966).

mental institution may compel a patient to perform work, provided that work was part of a therapeutic program and that the benefit to the patient outweighed the incidental labor requirement. However, if the work was "ruthless" and devoid of therapeutic benefit, then the forced labor could constitute involuntary servitude.

In applying *Jobson* to the mandatory community service programs, the *Immediato* district court recognized that the service program was not ruthless, did have educational purposes, and did teach a variety of real world skills, such as "cooperation, organization, and communication with others."[81] In short, because the nature of the required student service was in fact educational and was for the students' own benefit, the courts rejected the plaintiffs' claim that forced labor existed for the benefit of other people and that the labor lacked educational value.

In summary, in rejecting the claim that the mandatory community programs violated the Thirteenth Amendment, the courts took a "contextual approach"[82] and examined the "whole set of conditions"[83] presented to them. This contextual approach stood in contrast to the plain meaning approach which the plaintiffs requested the courts to apply.[84] (The plaintiffs had used not only the definition from *Bailey* quoted above[85] but also another, even earlier definition: voluntary servitude is "enforced compulsory service of one to another.")[86]

The courts' contextual approach thus constituted a rejection of the plaintiffs' plain meaning definitions and led to the three reasons offered by the courts: no level of physical or legal coercion akin to African slavery; existence of choices to avoid community service; and an education purpose of the programs for the students' own benefit. The courts adopted a consideration of the "general spirit"[87] of the term involuntary servitude though

---

[81] Immediato I, 873 F. Supp at 851.

[82] Steirer II, 987 F. 2d at 1000.

[83] *Id.* at 998.

[84] Herndon's Brief to the Fourth Circuit Court of Appeals at 29.

[85] 219 U.S. at 241.

[86] *Id.*

[87] The term comes from Kozminski, 487 U.S. at 942. Justice O'connor wrote, "While the general spirit of the phrase 'involuntary servitude' is easily comprehended, the exact range conditions it prohibits is harder to define." The district court in Herndon used this term (Herndon I, 899 F. Supp. at 1448) but did not attribute it to Kozminski. Subsequently neither did Herndon, objecting only that the district court, not the Supreme Court, had used an "amorphous standard." (Herndon's Brief to the Fourth Circuit Court of Appeals at 29).

the plaintiffs objected to such an approach. With this contextual approach the *Steirer II* court held that "[a]n educational requirement does not become involuntary servitude merely because one of the stated objectives of the Program is that the students will work 'without receiving pay.'"[88]

First Amendment Right of Freedom to Speak and Not to Speak

1. Plaintiffs' Claim of Violation of Freedom of Speech

The legal literature on First Amendment rights in general and freedom of speech rights in particular is vast and complex. It is within the context of numerous and well-known precedents that the plaintiffs challenged the constitutionality of the Bethlehem mandatory community service program[89] in regard to the First Amendment. The First Amendment, ratified effective December 15, 1791, states in its entirety:

> Congress shall make no law respecting an establishment of religion, or prohibiting the free exercise thereof; or abridging the freedom of speech, or of the press, or the right of the people peaceably to assemble, and to petition the Government for a redress of grievances. U.S. Const. Amend. I.

The challenge raised by the plaintiffs was "based upon their First Amendment right to refrain from engaging in speech or other symbolic gestures. The Courts of the United States have specifically recognized that this right exists within the context of students [sic] in our public school system."[90] In stating the claim as they did, the plaintiffs focused the courts' attention not on the commonly and popularly recognized right to speak but on the right not to speak, the right to remain silent. The plaintiffs cited and quoted from several cases decided by the Supreme Court, includ-

---

[88] Steirer II, 987 F. 2d at 1000.
[89] Only the Steirer plaintiffs challenged their program with a First Amendment violation. 937 F.2d at 993.
[90] Steirer's Brief in Support of Plaintiffs' Motion for Summary Judgment, United States District Court for the Eastern District of Pennsylvania at 16.

ing the school law case *Tinker v. Des Moines Independent Community School District.* [91]

The plaintiffs first noted that students maintain their constitutional rights while attending public schools. In *Tinker*, a case dealing with a student protest in December 1965, against the war in Vietnam, students wore black arm bands to express their opposition to the war. The Supreme Court reversed a lower court decision and upheld the students' constitutional right of free speech. Said the Court:

...It can hardly be argued that either students or teachers shed their constitutional rights to freedom of speech or expression at the schoolhouse gate. This has been the unmistakable holding of this Court for almost 50 years.[92]

The students also quoted the Court as saying, "The vigilant protection of constitutional freedoms is nowhere more vital than in the community of American schools."[93]

Then the plaintiffs claimed that the First Amendment protects not only the right to speak but, as importantly, the right to refrain from speaking or expressing a belief. The plaintiffs cited *Wooley v. Maynard*, a case that dealt with a First Amendment claim against displaying the New Hampshire state motto "Live Free or Die" on an automobile license plate so long as the plate still served the identification purpose.[94] The Supreme Court said in *Wooley* that the First Amendment "includes both the right to speak freely and the right to refrain from speaking at all."[95] In a later case dealing with professional fundraisers, the Court put it this way: "In the context of protected speech the difference between compelled speech and compelled silence is without constitutional significance, for the First Amendment guarantees 'freedom of speech,' a term necessarily comprising the decision of both what to say and what not to say."[96]

Finally, the plaintiffs showed that the right to refrain from speaking had been upheld in a school case. In *West Virginia State Board of Education v. Barnette*, a case dealing with a mandatory flag salute and the pledge of allegiance, a Jehovah Witness success-

---

[91] 393 U.S. 503, 89 S.Ct. 733, 21 L.Ed. 2d 731 (1969).
[92] *Id.* at 506
[93] Shelton v. Tucker, 364 U.S. 479, 487, 81 S.Ct. 247, 251, 5 L.Ed. 2d 231, 236-237 (1960).
[94] 430 U.S. 705, 97 S.Ct. 1428, 51 L.Ed. 2d 752 (1977).
[95] *Id.* at 714.
[96] Riley v. National Federation of the Blind, 487 U.S. 781, 796-797, 108 S.Ct. 2667, 2677, 101 L.Ed. 2d 669, 689 (1988).

fully claimed a violation of free speech in terms of the right to refrain from an act expressing a belief.[97] The Supreme Court supported the student, saying:

> That they ["the State itself and all of its creatures — Boards of Education not excepted"] are educating the young for citizenship is reason for scrupulous protection of Constitutional freedoms of the individual, if we are not to strangle the free mind at its source and teach youth to discount important principles of our government as mere platitudes....
> One's right to life, liberty, and property, to free speech, a free press, freedom of worship and assembly, and other fundamental rights may not be submitted to vote; they depend on the outcome of no elections....
> If there is any fixed star in our constitutional constellation, it is that no official, high or petty, can prescribe what shall be orthodox in politics, nationalism, religion, or other matters of opinion or force citizens to confess by word or act their faith therein.[98]

The plaintiffs claimed that the act of performing community service in the school's mandatory program was an expression of the belief in altruism. They claimed this in light of the statements made at the school board meeting at which the program was formally adopted by the defendant members of the board of education. The plaintiffs claimed that the defendants' statements indicated a particular reasoning and ideology that supported voting in favor of establishing the program. At a meeting on April 30, 1990, defendant board member Robert Thompson said:

> ...first of all, the proposal proclaims that like basic literacy, responsibility to the community which supports and nurtures them [students] is something we expect all young people to understand and practice....I believe we need to teach them that it is not just their privilege to volunteer if they feel so inclined but that as citizens of a democracy they have the responsibility to contribute something of their talent toward the welfare of the whole, to return to the community part of all that they have been given by the community....[99]

---

[97] 319 U.S. 624, 63 S.Ct. 1178, 87 L.Ed. 1628 (1943).
[98] *Id.* at 637, 638, and 642.
[99] Steirer's Brief of Appellants to the Third Circuit Court of Appeals at 19.

Defendant board member Uriel Trujillo said at the meeting:
"I, too, support the program as mandatory because...we do
have a duty to our community and we do have a responsibility to
each other...."[100]

In a deposition defendant board member John Spirk testified:
A: We owe it to our fellow man to help them out if we
can, if we have the time and know-how.
Q: In your view of the world it is right that people help
each other?
A: Oh, absolutely. I don't think there is enough of it.[101]

Quoting from the service program's stated objectives, from
statements made by board members at board meetings, and from
testimony given in discovery depositions about the reasons for
supporting the mandatory service program, the plaintiffs concluded that the "defendants who voted in favor of the Program
hold the belief that helping others has positive effects and is something to be proud of, i.e., that altruism is a desirable life
philosophy."[102] Thus, the plaintiffs claimed, students engage in
expressive conduct when performing community service due to
the altruistic ideological foundation of the program.

Finally, the plaintiffs claimed, based on the Due Process Clause
of the Fourteenth Amendment, that the applicable standard of review for their case was "the heightened level of scrutiny announced
in *Barnette* and *Tinker*...."[103] This heightened level of scrutiny, or
strict scrutiny, requires that a defendant demonstrate a compelling interest, not just a legitimate one, in implementing the
requirement under consideration.

In summary, the plaintiff students claimed that they "should
be free to opt out of a program that requires them to affirm by
their actions a life philosophy proclaimed by the appellee school
directors, particularly when allowing such an option would not
substantially impair or interfere with the appellee school district's
ability to function."[104] They claimed that the community service
program because of its ideological base and its mandatory status
"impinged" on their First Amendment right "to refrain from co-

---

[100] *Id.* at 21.
[101] *Id.* at 22.
[102] Steirer's Brief in Support of Plaintiffs' Motion, *supra* note 56, at 21.
[103] *Id.* at 32.
[104] Steirer's Brief of Appellants to the Third Circuit Court of Appeals at 14.

erced conduct which affirms an idealogical [sic] viewpoint or set of values propagated [sic] by a Government official."[105]

2. The Courts' Response to Plaintiffs' Claim of Freedom of Speech

The Third Circuit appellate court readily accepted the plaintiffs' position that the First Amendment freedom of speech includes both the right to speak and the right to refrain from speaking or making other symbolic, expressive gestures. It also accepted the defendants' position that a local board of education has broad discretion as to what should be the curriculum of a school under its control. The court said, "The Supreme Court has noted that '[s]tates and local school boards are generally afforded considerable discretion in operating public schools.'"[106] However, the court did not accept the idea, implied by the defendants, that because the service program had an established and acknowledged educational purpose the program was automatically constitutional.[107] The court maintained that the teaching of values, which was a purpose of the service program and a purpose of virtually every part of the high school curriculum, still "must conform to constitutional standards."[108]

Therefore, in light of the *Barnette* precedent of the Supreme Court that the symbolic act of saluting the flag and reciting the pledge was a form of utterance, the legal issue became "whether the performance of community service as a required school program carries with it the same 'affirmation of a belief and attitude of mind' that is a prerequisite for First Amendment protection" (quoting *Barnette*, 319 U.S. at 633).[109]

The Third Circuit appellate court first distinguished the act of performing community service from the acts in question in prior cases that included an "obviously expressive element."[110] Such acts, which were held to be protected by the First Amendment

---

[105] *Id.*

[106] Steirer II, 987 F.2d at 993, quoting Edwards v. Aguillard, 482 U.S. 578, 583, 107 S.Ct. 2573, 96 L.Ed.2d 510 (1987).

[107] Steirer II, 987 F.2d at 994.

[108] *Id.*

[109] *Id.*

[110] *Id.* at 995.

because of the expressive element, included the displaying of the motto "Live Free or Die" on an automobile license plate,[111] contributing money to the teachers' labor union for the purpose of political lobbying and persuasion,[112] wearing a black arm band to protest the Vietnam War,[113]and the burning of a draft card.[114] In the first two instances above people claimed the right to refrain from such expressive activity; in the last two, people claimed the right to express themselves with such conduct.

On the other hand, the Third Circuit recognized that because not all acts may be labeled as speech with an expressive element, case decisions exist where the acts in question were deemed not to be protected by the First Amendment. The court cited and quoted from *City of Dallas v. Stanglin*,[115] a case dealing with recreational roller-skating dancing in a roller rink. The Supreme Court in that case had ruled that the dance-hall patrons had not engaged in "expressive association" and indicated that the expressive element needed for First Amendment protection is a matter of degree in that virtually every human act is expressive. The Supreme Court contended that:

> it is possible to find some kernel of expression in almost every activity a person undertakes—for example, walking down the street or meeting one's friends at a shopping mall—but such a kernel is not sufficient to bring the activity within the protection of the First Amendment.[116]

The *Steirer II* court, thus, recognized that in searching for a way to decide whether mandatory community service constitutes expressive conduct it had to look at the activity itself and the "factual context and environment in which it is undertaken."[117] To guide its look at the nature of the activity and its context the court turned to a test established by the Supreme Court in *Spence v. Washington*,[118] a case that dealt with the displaying of the American flag upside down with a peace symbol attached to the front and back

---

[111] Riley, 487 U.S. 781.

[112] Abood v. Detroit Bd. of Education, 431 U.S. 209, 97 S.Ct. 1782, 52 L.Ed. 2d 261 (1977).

[113] Tinker, 393 U.S. 503.

[114] United States v. O'Brien, 391, U.S. 367, 88 S.Ct., 1673, 20 L.Ed. 2d 672 (1968).

[115] 490 U.S. 19, 109 S.Ct. 1591, 104 L.Ed. 2d 18 (1989).

[116] *Id*. at 25.

[117] Steirer II, 987 F.2d at 995. Thus the appellate court took a contextual approach for adjudicating both claims brought to it.

[118] 418 U.S. 405, 94 S.Ct. 2727, 41 L.Ed. 2d 841 (1974).

made of black tape, covering about half of the surface of the flag. The displayer was a college student who hung the flag from his apartment window on private property in Seattle, Washington.

According to the two-prong *Spence* test, an act is protected by the First Amendment if it is "sufficiently imbued with elements of communication." It is so (1)when the actor has "an intent to convey a particularized message" and (2)when in the "surrounding circumstances" the likelihood is great that the message will "be understood" by those who view it.[119] In applying the *Spence* test to mandatory community service, the *Steirer* courts concluded that the expressive element is absent in two ways. First, the students were not required to express a belief in altruism or the goodness of helping the community either orally or in writing their feedback reports. (See Figures 1-7.) Nor were the students required to serve one particular organization selected by school officials. On the contrary, the students were able to select their own avenue of service from "a multitude of service options" or to design their own compatible "experiential situation."[120]

Second, the *Steirer* courts found no evidence that community people who witnessed students performing their service were likely to understand that the students were expressing a particularized belief in altruism. Community people, said the courts, would likely understand that students were simply fulfilling a school curricular requirement similar to doing homework or to exercising in the gymnasium in physical education class. For the courts, the community service program was similar to a drug education program or a family life-sex education program that "schools have traditionally undertaken to point students toward values generally shared by the community."[121] The courts concluded that students could participate in such service programs without expressing a belief in them despite their ideological foundation. In short, the performance of community service, as designed by the school's program, was held to be non-expressive. Because there was no expression of belief, the courts saw no need to consider the Fourteen Amendment issue of whether the government had a compelling interest in implementing the mandatory community service program.

---

[119] *Id.* at 409, 410-411.
[120] Steirer II, 987 F.2d at 996.
[121] *Id.* at 997.

The *Steirer* courts recognized and supported the position that schools teach values to students as they take their places in community life. The appellate court noted that the Supreme Court has embraced the notion that schools teach values for that is one of the charges to the schools. The teaching of values was the crux of the matter not only in *Barnette* and *Tinker, supra,* but also in *Ambach v. Norwick,* a case dealing with a citizenship requirement for teachers in New York public schools.[122] In *Ambach* the Supreme Court said that schools are important "in the preservation of the values on which our society rests" and for "inculcating fundamental values necessary to the maintenance of a democratic political system."[123]

The *Steirer* courts also explicitly noted from two other Supreme Court decisions that (1) education is the responsibility of teachers, parents, and state and local government rather than that of the federal courts";[124] and (2) that courts "do not and cannot intervene in the resolution of conflicts which arise in the daily operation of school systems and which do not directly and sharply implicate constitutional values."[125]

Based on such direction from the Supreme Court the *Steirer* courts rejected the plaintiffs' First and Fourteenth Amendment claims as lacking merit, saying, "The mere fact that the course content itself reflects a particular ideology does not necessarily trench upon First Amendment proscriptions."[126]

---

[122] 441 U.S. 68, 99 S.Ct. 1589, 60 L.Ed. 2d 49 (1979).

[123] *Id.* at 77. *See also* Bethel School Dist. 403 v. Fraser, 478 U.S. 675, 106 S.Ct. 3159, 92 L.Ed. 2d 549 (1986); Board of Education, Island Trees Union Free School District No. 26 v. Pico, 457 U.S. 853, 102 S.Ct. 2799, 73 L.Ed. 2d 435 (1982).

[124] Steirer I, 789 F.Supp. at 1347, citing Hazelwood Sch. Dist. v. Kuhlmeier, 484 U.S. 260, 273, 108 S.Ct. 562, 571, 98 L.Ed. 2d 592, 606-607 (1988). *See also* Milliken v. Bradley, 418 U.S. 717, 744, 94 S.Ct. 3112, 3127, 41 L.Ed. 2d 1069, 1090-1091(1974).

[125] Steirer II, 987 F.2d at 994, quoting Epperson v. Arkansas, 393 U.S. 97, 104, 89 S.Ct. 266, 270, 21 L.Ed. 2d 228, 234 (1966).

[126] *Id.*

Fourteenth Amendment Parental Liberty Right

1. Plaintiffs' Claim of Violation of Parental Liberty Right to Direct Their Children's Education

The plaintiffs claimed that under the Ninth Amendment[127] and the Due Process Clause of the Fourteenth Amendment parents have a liberty "right to direct and control the upbringing and education of the children in accord with their own views."[128]

The Ninth Amendment in its entirety states, "The enumeration in the Constitution of certain rights shall not be construed to deny or disparage others retrained by the people."

The Fourteenth Amendment in pertinent part states. "No state shall make or enforce any law which shall abridge the privileges or immunities of citizens of the United States; nor shall any state deprive any person of life, liberty, or property without due process of law...."

According to the plaintiff parents, the schools violated the constitution by intruding into the relationship between parents and their children by mandating the requirement to participate in a community service program. The parents objected to the service program on secular values, not religious grounds, believing that people are not obligated to help others.[129]

The parental liberty right stems from well-known Supreme Court cases. In *Meyer v. Nebraska,* a case dealing with the teaching of a modern foreign language to ten-year old children who had not yet passed the eighth grade, the Supreme Court supported the right of the teacher (Meyer) to teach German and the right of the parents to direct their child's education.[130] The Court considered the "civic development" purpose of Nebraska's statute to "inhibit training and education" of children in "foreign tongues

---

[127] The plaintiffs claimed that their right is secured under the Ninth and Fourteenth Amendments. However, their subsequent briefs to the courts did not rely on any Ninth Amendment precedents. Thus, the parents and then the courts treated this claim of parental liberty only on a Fourteenth Amendment basis.

[128] Complaint filed by Immediato and Gironda families in U.S. District Court, Southern Division of N.Y., Count II, ¶26, April 19, 1994.

[129] Immediato I, 873 F.Supp. at 851, n.4 and 5.

[130] 262 U.S. 390, 43 S.Ct. 625, 67 L.Ed. 1042 (1923).

and ideals" before learning "English and acquiring American ideals."[131] The Court ruled that:

> the state may do much, go very far, indeed, in order to improve the quality of its citizens, physically, mentally, and morally....but [the understanding of our ordinary speech] cannot be coerced by methods which conflict with the Constitution—a desirable end cannot be promoted by prohibited means.[132]

In *Pierce v. Society of Sisters*, a case which dealt with the right of the State of Oregon (Pierce was the governor) to require that parents educate their children ages 8-16 in a public school,[133] the Supreme Court again supported the "liberty of parents and guardians to direct the upbringing and education of children under their control."[134] The Court stated:

> The fundamental theory of liberty upon which all governments in this Union repose excludes any general power of the state to standardize its children by forcing them to accept instruction from public teachers only. The child is not the mere creature of the state; those who nurture him and direct his destiny have the right, coupled with the high duty, to recognize and prepare him for additional obligations.[135]

The Supreme Court reaffirmed this parental liberty in *Wisconsin v. Yoder*,[136] a case dealing with the rights of Amish parents who decided not to send their children to school beyond the eighth grade. While recognizing that the Amish parents based their legal claim in the religion clauses of the First Amendment and not on the parental rights component of the Fourteenth Amendment, the Court did speak of the role of parents in the education of their children:

> The history and culture of Western civilization reflect a strong tradition of parental concerns for the nurture and upbringing of their children. This primary role of parents in the upbringing of their children is now established beyond debate as an enduring American tradition.[137]

---

[131] *Id*. at 401.
[132] *Id*.
[133] 268 U.S. 510, 45 S.Ct. 571, 69 L.Ed. 1070 (1925).
[134] *Id*. at 534.
[135] *Id*. at 535.
[136] 406 U.S. 205, 92 S.Ct. 1526, 32 L.Ed. 2d 15 (1972).
[137] *Id*. at 232.

In addition to asserting their parental liberty right, the plaintiffs claimed that this right was a fundamental one. Moreover, they claimed, their parental liberty right was a fundamental one under the Fourteenth Amendment without needing to be based in or combined with the religion clause of the First Amendment. "Parental Rights are fundamental and need not be religiously-based to be protected under the Fourteenth Amendment."[138] To support their claim the parents cited a Massachusetts Supreme Judicial Court case[139] and a New York case,[140] which recognized the parental right as fundamental in two cases dealing with condom distribution in high school. "Parents possess a fundamental liberty interest, protected by the Fourteenth Amendment, to be free from unnecessary intrusion in the rearing of their children."[141]

The parents argued that even though *Meyer* and *Pierce* courts applied the rational basis test when reviewing the requirements set by the States of Nebraska and Oregon, the correct standard for their community service cases in the 1990s was strict scrutiny. The two-tiered framework first appeared a decade and a half after *Meyer* when the Supreme Court established its current modern rational basis review, a standard deferential to legislators.[142] That is to say, the term "reasonable" as used in *Meyer* and *Pierce*, is significantly different from the "reasonable" modern standard.

"Although both cases [*Meyer* and *Pierce*] use the term "reasonable," they were decided over a decade before the U.S. Supreme Court established its current standards of review in *United States v. Caroline Products*, 304 U.S. 144, 152 n.4 (1938) (setting forth modern "rational basis" review). Indeed, if the Court had applied the highly lax rational basis standard, it likely would have upheld the challenged statutes in *Meyer* and *Pierce*."[143]

The effect of this plaintiff claim was to request the courts to subject the school's service requirement to strict scrutiny, a heightened level of review. If the court would agree to apply such a

---

[138] Herndon's Brief to the Fourth Circuit Court of Appeals at 7.
[139] Curtis v. School Committee of Falmouth, 420 Mass. 749, 652 N.E. 2d 580 (1995).
[140] Alfonso v. Fernandez, 606 N.Y.S. 2d 259, 265-67 (A.D. 2 Dept. 1993), appeal dismissed without op., 614 N.Y.S. 2d 388 (1994). The court did not say explicitly that the parental right is fundamental. It said only that violation of the parental right requires "an overriding necessity" by the government. *Id.* at 265.
[141] Curtis, 652 N.E. 2d 585. Although the court said that the parental right was fundamental, the court held that condum distribution availability does not burden the parents.
[142] United States v. Caroline Products Co., 304 U.S. 144, 58 S.Ct. 778, 82, L.Ed. 1234, (1938).
[143] Herndon's Brief to the Fourth Circuit Court of Appeals at 10.

high standard when reviewing the requirement, the school then would have to demonstrate a "compelling governmental interest" in the service program in order to overcome the parents' right. (The plaintiffs asserted that the school could not do so.) Based on this claim, the plaintiff parents requested the courts to hold the mandatory service programs to be unconstitutional or, in the alternative, to permit the parents to exempt their children from the programs.[144]

In seeking approval of an "opt-out" provision from the court the parents made a distinction between what the schools teach via demonstration or words ("merely teach or expose") and what the schools teach via having students learn through actions. The parents did accept the legitimacy of teaching their students even "objectionable values" in recognition of the state's interest in their children's education. However, the parents opposed the teaching of values that were contrary to their values if that teaching required the students to learn by taking actions. So as to protect the parents' right from court interference the parents suggested the following balancing rule: "If public schools merely teach or expose children to objectionable values, parents normally cannot claim a violation of their right to direct their children's education. However, public schools cannot force students to take actions contrary to their parents' values."[145]

In formulating and offering the balancing rule the parents relied on uncited "early common law cases" and in particular on *Mozert v. Hawkins County Board of Education.*[146] *Mozert* was a 1987 Sixth Circuit case dealing with a parental request, based on the Free Exercise of Religion Clause of the First Amendment, where the parents sought to exempt their children from reading classes that used the Holt, Rinehart and Winston basic reading series. In that case the district court granted an opt-out provision, but on appeal the Sixth Circuit Court of Appeals reversed the lower court decision. In discussing the testimony and the district court's reasoning, the appellate court made a distinction between a student reading and discussing the objectionable material in the textbook and the student being required to "act out" certain points in ac-

---

[144] Complaint, *supra* note 128, filed for Immediato I, Count II, ¶28 and parents' briefs to the Immediato and Herndon courts.

[145] Herndon's Brief to the Fourth Circuit Court of Appeals at 14.

[146] 827 F.2d 1058 (6th Cir. 1987), *cert. denied*, 484 U.S. 1066 (1988).

tivities suggested in the teachers' manuals. As summarized by the parents in their brief, the Sixth Circuit Court of Appeals concluded that participation " 'beyond reading and discussing assigned materials' would raise constitutional concerns 'because the element of compulsion would then be present'" in the classroom.[147]

2. The Courts' Response to the Parental Liberty Claim

The *Immediato* and *Herndon* courts readily accepted the parents' contention that a parental liberty right exists. "Parents, of course, have a liberty interest, properly cognizable under the Fourteenth Amendment, in the upbringing of their children."[148] Therefore, the courts had to decide for the first time in these community service cases whether to use a heightened level of review or a rational basis standard of review. With the Thirteenth Amendment Claim they did not have to decide such a question because involuntary servitude is explicitly mentioned in the constitution. Nor did the *Steirer* courts have a need to decide such a question about level of review with the First Amendment free speech claim because they had decided that performing community service was not expressive of a belief and not protected by the First Amendment.

While the courts readily accepted that a parental liberty right exists, they did not accept quickly and without much discussion the contention that the parental liberty right before them, invoked on secular grounds, constituted a fundamental right deserving of a heightened level of review rather than the low, rational basis review. (Under a heightened level of review, or strict scrutiny review, courts require the government to demonstrate that its regulation being challenged is narrowly tailored to serve a compelling state interest. Under the low, rational basis test for a non-fundamental right (that is, the "impairment of a lesser interest"), the government need only show that its regulation is a "reasonable fit" between the "governmental purpose" and "the means to advance that purpose."[149]

---

[147] Herndon's Brief to the Sixth Circuit Court of Appeals 17, quoting *Mozert*, 827 F.2d at 1064.
[148] Immediato II, 73 F. 3d at 461.
[149] *Id*. at 460-461, quoting from Reno v. Flores, 507 U.S. 292, 305, 113 S.Ct. 1439, 1443-1449, 123 L.Ed. 2d 1, 18-19 (1993).

Moreover, the *Immediato* and *Herndon* courts recognized that the plaintiffs' claim of the existence of a fundamental parental liberty right based on secular values and the request for applying a heightened level of scrutiny to the community service requirement presented a legal challenge to them. The courts realized that to uphold the claim and to honor the request for a strict scrutiny review they would have "to break new ground" in constitutional law in that there was no Supreme Court precedent declaring the parental liberty right as fundamental. For this reason the courts proceeded with "humility and caution."[150]

Thus, after accepting the existence of the parental liberty right as found in the Supreme Court decisions of *Meyer, Pierce, Yoder,* and *Farrington v. Tokushige*[151] (dealing with the Hawaiian statute restricting schools teaching in a language other than English or Hawaiian), the courts focused their attention on the appropriate level of review to apply to the service program requirement. First, the courts noted that the Supreme Court never has indicated explicitly whether the parental right is fundamental.[152] Next, the courts reviewed the pertinent decisions of the Supreme Court in regard to the exact language of the Court and the standard used for reaching a decision.

The *Immediato* and *Herndon* courts determined that the standard for reviewing parental liberty rights was the rational basis review by which the Supreme Court asked whether the governmental requirement under consideration was "reasonable." The courts cited five cases in which the reasonable standard appeared: *Meyer,* where the Supreme Court held that the Nebraska statute was "arbitrary and without reasonable relation to any end within the competency of the state";[153] *Pierce,* where the Supreme Court found that the statute had "no reasonable relation to some purpose within the competency of the State";[154] *Tokushige,* where the Supreme Court said that a "Japanese parent has the right to direct the education of his own child without unreasonable restrictions";[155] *Yoder,* where the Supreme Court in discussing parental

---

[150] *Id.* at 461.
[151] 273 U.S. 284, 47 S.Ct. 406, 71 L.Ed. 646 (1927).
[152] Immediato II, 73 F. 3d at 461.
[153] *Id.,* quoting Meyer, 262 U.S. at 403.
[154] *Id.,* quoting Pierce, 268 U.S. at 535; Herndon II quotes Pierce at 534, (statute "unreasonably interferes" with parental right; and see Pierce at 534 ("No question is raised concerning the power of the state reasonably to regulate all schools....").
[155] Herndon II, 89 F.3d at 178, quoting Tokushige, 273 U.S at 298.

rights combined with First Amendment religious rights, said, "A way of life, however virtuous and admirable, may not be interposed as a barrier to reasonable state regulation of education if it is based on purely secular considerations";[156] and *Runyon v. McCrary* (a case dealing with racial discrimination in a private nonsectarian school), where the Supreme Court stated that parents "have no constitutional right to provide their children with education unfettered by reasonable government regulation."[157]

The courts acknowledged that *Meyer, Pierce,* and *Tokushige* all were decided before the Supreme Court created the two tiered framework and at a time when it "used only the 'traditional' standard of scrutiny."[158] Nevertheless, the courts concluded upon inspecting the pertinent Supreme Court decisions concerning the parental liberty right that the appropriate standard of review was the rational basis "except when the parents' interest include[d] a religious element."[159] Therefore, the courts decided to apply a rational basis review to the mandatory community service programs because the plaintiffs based their complaints on secular, not religious, values alone.

Only the *Immediato* district court responded explicitly to the opt-out request. First, the court simply restated the parents' assertion that the parents should have the "ability to have their children opt out of programs that are contrary to the beliefs and values they seek to impart."[160] Then the court said only that it found "no federal case law" to support the request "to opt out of an educational curriculum for purely secular reasons."[161] The Second Circuit appellate court only alluded to the parents' opt-out request by commenting on the distinction proposed between teaching by words or exposure and teaching by action. That court rejected the distinction, saying that the "exposure/action distinction is somewhat chimerical, particularly in the educational context. In the course of education, schools often require more than a passive glance at a book."[162] The court then went on to

---

[156] *Id.,* quoting Yoder 406 U.S. at 215.
[157] Immediato II, 73 F. 3d at 461, quoting Runyon v. McCrary, 427 U.S. 160, 178, 96 S.Ct. 2586, 2598, 49 L.Ed. 2d 415, 429 (1976).
[158] Herndon II, 89 F. 3d at 178.
[159] *Id.* at 179.
[160] Immediato's Memorandum in Support of Motion for Summary Judgment 22.
[161] Immediato I, 873 F.Supp. at 852. The only case law found was based on New York State health services law. *See* Alfonso, 606 N.Y.S. 2d 259.
[162] Immediato II, 73 F.3d at 462.

state that even if the distinction were valid in education, it would then bear on whether the state requirement meets the standard of review, not on whether the standard of review should be rational basis or strict scrutiny.[163] The *Herndon* courts did not deal with the opt-out request explicitly or even by allusion.

With a conclusion to use the rational basis standard based on their review of Supreme Court decisions combined with a quick or silent rejection of the opt-out request, the *Immediato* and *Herndon* courts then asked whether the mandatory programs were reasonably related to the educational purposes of the schools. Here the conclusion of the courts was that the service programs "easily"[164] met the rational basis test and did "not infringe unconstitutionally"[165] on the parents' right to direct their children's upbringing and education. One role of the schools is to teach values, some of which might well conflict with the parents' values in that, as the courts recognized, everything that a school decides to include in its curriculum is a value judgment. The value judgment behind mandatory community service "is not materially different from that of underlying programs that seek to discourage drug use and premature sexual activity, encourage knowledge of civics and abiding in the rule of law, and even encourage good eating habits. Schools have traditionally undertaken to point students toward values generally shared by the community."[166] These decisions to teach generally accepted community values do not deny parents the right to direct the upbringing of their children.

Furthermore, even though some of the values of the parents do conflict with the values taught by the school, the *Immediato* district court refused to intervene and to "usurp the legitimate authority" of the duly elected officials engaged in educating citizens.[167] The courts accepted the Supreme Court's decision not to intervene in conflicts arising in the daily operation of the schools.[168] The *Immediato* district court put it this way. "To attempt to do so [usurp legitimate authority] because we or Plaintiffs consider the Program undesirable on purely secular grounds would wreak havoc in the administration of the schools, and involve the federal judiciary impermissibly in matters of local Home Rule."[169]

---

[163] *Id.*
[164] Immediato II, 73 F. 3d at 462.
[165] Herndon II, 89 F. 3d at 179.
[166] Steirer II, 987 F. 2d at 997.
[167] Immediato I, 873 F. Supp. at 852.
[168] Epperson, 393 U.S. at 104.
[169] Immediato I, 873 F. Supp. at 852.

The courts pointed out that the state, too, has a legitimate interest in the education of children, which interest deserves consideration along with the parents' interest. To support their conclusion in favor of the schools' efforts to teach citizenship values the courts cited three Supreme Court decisions. In *Brown v. Topeka Board of Education*, the well known 1954 segregation case, the Court unanimously stated that "education is perhaps the most important function of the state,"[170] as it declared an end to racial segregation in schools.

The courts also cited *Yoder* where the Supreme Court, while holding for the parents, indicated that the state does have a "compelling" interest in the education of children, but that it does not overcome the First Amendment rights of the Amish.[171]

"The State advances two primary arguments in support of compulsory education. It notes, as Thomas Jefferson pointed out early in our history, that some degree of education is necessary to prepare citizens to participate effectively and intelligently in our open political system if we are to preserve freedom and independence. Further, education prepares individuals to be self-reliant and self-sufficient participants in society. We accept these propositions."[172]

Finally, the Second Circuit appellate court, referring to *Ambach*, also stated, "The state's interest in education extends to teaching students the values and habits of good citizenship, and introducing them to their social responsibilities as citizens."[173] In sum, because the schools through the vehicle of the mandatory community service program sought to further the states' interest and objectives in education in a reasonable manner, there was no violation of the parents' liberty right claimed under the Ninth and Fourteenth Amendments.

---

[170] 347 U.S. 483, 493, 74 S.Ct. 686, 98 L.Ed. 2d 873 (1954).
[171] Yoder, 406 U.S. at 221.
[172] *Id.*
[173] Immediato II, 73 F. 3d at 462, citing Ambach, 441 U.S. at 80.

Fourteenth Amendment Student Personal Liberty Right

1. Plaintiffs' Claim of Violation of the Students' Personal Liberty Right

The plaintiffs claimed that under the substantive component of the Due Process Clause of the Fourteenth Amendment they have a personal liberty right.[174] For the students this liberty right pertains to the ability to determine on their own when they will perform community service. The students claimed that "within the range of personal decisions protected by the Fourteenth Amendment must be the right to determine whether an individual wishes to provide charitable service to others."[175]

The students further claimed that the community service program violated tradition as embodied in the common law. "The school district's requirement of service to others is directly contrary to the long-established common law principle of refusing to transform what many would consider a moral duty (service to others) into a state-imposed obligation."[176] The community service task, they claimed, is different from other tasks required by schools, such as attendance at school and taking tests to demonstrate proficiencies. The difference lies in the performing of "uncompensated, charitable service to others as a condition of graduation."[177]

The plaintiffs admitted that this claim raised an issue of first impression for the courts and that a consequence of being first with any claim was the lack of case law to support that claim.[178] Therefore, they supported their claim by connecting it to the list of items in *Meyer* that have been acknowledged definitely as being part of the definition of the term liberty.[179]

---

[174] *See* prior section for the quotation from the pertinent part of the Fourteenth Amendment.

[175] Herndon's Brief to the Fourth Circuit Court of Appeals at 22. *See* same assertion in Immediato's Brief to the Second Circuit Court of Appeals at 19 except for the omission of the word "charitable" there.

[176] *Id.* at 23.

[177] *Id.* at 22.

[178] *Id.* and Immediato's Brief to the Second Circuit Court of Appeals at 19.

[179] Meyer, 262 U.S. at 399.

In referring to the aspect of liberty protected by the Fourteenth Amendment, the Court in *Meyer* indicated:

> While this court has not attempted to define with exactness the liberty thus guaranteed, the term has received much consideration and some of the included things have been definitely stated. Without doubt, it denotes not merely freedom from bodily restraint but also the right of the individual to contract, to engage in any of the occupations of life, to acquire useful knowledge, to marry, establish a home and bring up children, to worship God according to the dictates of his own conscience, and generally to enjoy the privileges long recognized at common law as essential to the orderly pursuit of happiness by free men[180]

In light of the Supreme Court's statement about the definition of the term liberty, the plaintiffs did "not seek the creation of a new constitutional right," but rather sought only the recognition of student decision-making about personal matters, such as performing community service , as one of the privileges referred to in *Meyer*. If so recognized by the courts, the performance of community service would become the result of personal decision-making and individual choice as one of the "privileges long recognized at common law." Such a privilege could not then be commanded by a government requirement because it would be included already within the concept of liberty guaranteed by the Fourteenth Amendment.[181] The plaintiffs maintained that performing community service has traditionally been a matter of "individual conscience and belief."[182]

Furthermore, the plaintiffs claimed that the mandatory community service requirement not only violated the students' Fourteenth Amendment personal liberty right but that it did so without a compelling interest. "Deprivation of liberty may be justified only by a compelling governmental interest."[183] Thus, the

---

[180] *Id.*

[181] Herndon's Brief, to the Fourth Circuit Court of Appeals at 23-24 and Immediato's Brief to the Second Circuit Court of Appeals at 20.

[182] *Id.*

[183] Herndon's Complaint filed in the United States District Court for the Middle District of North Carolina, Count III, ¶34, April 19, 1994 and Immediato's Complaint filed in the United States District Court for the Southern District of New York, Count III, ¶33, April 19, 1994.

plaintiffs requested the courts to employ a strict scrutiny test when reviewing this claim and argued that the school districts' educational interests "do not rise to the level of significant or compelling such that they override students' liberty rights."[184]

2. The Courts' Response to the Plaintiffs' Claim of Violation of the Students' Personal Liberty Right

As with the claim for violation of the parental liberty right, the *Immediato* and *Herndon* courts recognized that to accept the claim of violation of the students' personal liberty right and to uphold that claim would involve breaking new ground. The courts would have to hold that the students had a liberty right protected under the substantive component of the Fourteenth Amendment's Due Process Clause and that this right was a fundamental one deserving of a strict scrutiny review. The *Immediato II* court decided to "decline plaintiffs' invitation to be the first court to so hold."[185]

That court admitted that it was "reluctant to expand the concept of substantive due process," following a recent Supreme Court admonition to that effect.[186] Also, it recognized that the Supreme Court had granted substantive due process to protect only those rights that it deemed implicate personal freedoms "implicit in the concept of ordered liberty."[187] The courts reviewed prior Court statements about substantive due process and then concluded that the students' claim did not involve decisions that met the criteria set forth by the Supreme Court, whether the criteria are stated as personal freedoms implicit in the concept of ordered liberty,[188] or "the most intimate and personal choices a person may make in a lifetime, choices central to personal dignity and autonomy,"[189] or "liberties expressly protected by the Bill of Rights."[190] That is to say, the courts maintained that not every liberty right is a fundamental right under the Due Process Clause.

---

[184] Herndon's Brief, to the Fourth Circuit Court of Appeals.

[185] Immediato II, 73 F. 3d at 463.

[186] *Id.*, quoting Collins v. City of Harker Heights, 503 U.S. 115, 125, 112 S.Ct. 1061, 1068-1069, 117 L.Ed. 2d 261, 273 (1992).

[187] *See* Palko v. Connecticut, 302 U.S. 319, 325, 58 S.Ct. 119, 151-152, 82 L.Ed. 288, 292 1937.

[188] *Id.*

[189] Herndon II, 89 F. 3d at 180, quoting Planned Parenthood v. Casey, 505 U.S. 833, 851, 112 S.Ct. 2791, 2806-2807,120 L.Ed. 2d 674, 698 (1992).

[190] Id. at 179-180.

Furthermore, the courts commented on and rejected the logic presented by the plaintiffs. The courts did not contest the existence of a personal liberty right. Rather, they began with the point that the plaintiffs offered a claim about community service that admittedly had no precedent. They acknowledged that the claim rested on a long-established common law principle that a moral duty does not entail a governmental obligation to perform the duty. However, the Fourth Circuit appellate court pointed out that "the absence of a common law duty does not imply a constitutional prohibition against the imposition of such a duty" by a public school board of education.[191] In recognition of this point about the flaw in the plaintiffs' logic the courts rejected the common law basis of the plaintiffs' personal liberty claim.

In sum, the courts held that the students' personal liberty right was not a fundamental one and did not require a heightened level of review but only a rational basis test. The courts refused to expand the substantive reach of the Fourteenth Amendment and decided, since the service programs met the rational basis review, to reject the students' personal liberty claim. The students' decisions to perform community service were "not the stuff to which strict scrutiny is devoted,"[192] thereby not meriting Fourteenth Amendment protection. Nor did the courts credit the common law argument. The students did not set forth a convincing personal liberty claim.

Fourteenth Amendment Student Privacy Right

1. Plaintiffs' Claim of Violation of Students' Privacy Right

The student plaintiffs claimed that the mandatory community service programs violated their privacy rights as found in the substantive components of the Fourteenth Amendment's Due Process Clause and in the Ninth Amendment. The students claimed that the violation of the rights occurred because the programs require participants "to choose a particular service activity and to reveal

---

[191] Id. at 179.
[192] Immediato II, 73 F.3d at 463.

and document" to the school the names of the organization and the activities performed for them.[193] The students desired to keep the requested information private in that they believed that their choices of service activity involved expressions of personal moral or political opinions.[194]

They argued:

> The type of community service one performs is an inherently personal choice, deeply reflective of an individual's "concept of the good." In deciding where and how to volunteer, an individual must choose what causes or organizations are most important to him or her and most worthy of one's time and energies. This choice inevitably reflects underlying moral and political value judgments.[195]

As shown by Figure 8 (page 62), the students brought this claim to both *Immediato* courts but only to the *Herndon* district court.

The students grounded their claims in the Supreme Court's statement in *Whalen v. Roe*, a case dealing with a New York State requirement that prescriptions for dangerous legitimate drugs be prepared on an official form (*Whalen* was the Commissioner of Health of New York).[196] *Whalen* identified a negative and a positive privacy right, that is, a right to avoid disclosure of important personal information and a right to make important decision on one's own. In referring to prior pertinent cases Justice Stevens wrote, "The cases sometimes characterized as protecting 'privacy' have in fact involved at least two different kinds of interests. One is the individual interest in avoiding disclosure of personal matters, and another is the interest in independence in making certain kinds of important decisions."[197]

The plaintiffs also grounded their claim in religion (though they did not mention the First Amendment anywhere in this privacy claim). They stated that religious students in general are in a dilemma about revealing their religious beliefs and that *Herndon*, in particular as a Christian, "believe[s] that charitable deeds should be private and shared only with the recipients of Christian charity."[198] Thus, not only were the students being forced to reveal

---

[193] Complaint filed by Immediato, in the district court at Count IV, ¶36.
[194] *Id.* at ¶37.
[195] Immediato's Memorandum in Support of Motion for Summary Judgment 40.
[196] 429 U.S. 589, 97 S.Ct. 869, 51 L.Ed. 64 (1977).
[197] *Id.* at 598-600.
[198] Herndon's Memorandum in Support of Plaintiffs' Motion for Summary Judgment 43.

service activity that should be kept secret, but they were also being forced to reveal their religious beliefs.

Not only did the students claim violation of their individual interests against disclosure ("confidentiality") and independence in decision-making ("autonomy") but they also claimed that the mandated disclosure "chills" their ability to exercise their constitutional rights.[199]

Furthermore, the students requested that the courts apply more than a rational basis test when they review the requirements set for the service programs by the local boards of education. They requested that the service programs "must be justified, at a minimum, by 'substantial' governmental interests,"[200] citing the approach used in *Barry v. City of New York*, a case dealing with the disclosure of financial information relating to the status of one's health.[201] The students also relied upon *Walls v. City of Petersburg*, another case involving, in part, disclosure of financial information.[202] In that case the court held that privacy rights were protected against the government's interest in financial information where the defendants had "the burden to prove that a compelling government interest in disclosure outweighs the individual privacy interest."[203]

In short, the plaintiffs claimed that there were "no compelling or substantial governmental interests to require students to reveal and document" where and what they performed for their community service.[204] Thus, they asked the court to protect the privacy of the students as guaranteed by the Ninth and Fourteenth Amendments.

2. The Courts' Response to the Plaintiffs' Claim of Violation of Student's Privacy Rights

The Second Circuit was the only appellate court to deal with the students' claim of a Fourteenth Amendment substantive due process privacy right. (See Figure 8, page 62.) Steirer never raised

---

[199] Immediato's Memorandum, to the district court at 39 and 44.
[200] *Id*. at 45.
[201] 712 F.2d 1554 (2d Cir. 1983).
[202] 895 F.2d 188 (4th Cir. 1990).
[203] *Id*. at 192.
[204] Herndon's Memorandum in Support of Plaintiffs' Motion for Summary Judgment 46.

this claim, and Herndon dropped it in his appeal, as noted explicitly by the Fourth Circuit Court of Appeals.[205] The student privacy claim is the only one of the five claims that was not appealed after being lost in a district court. It is also the only one of the five claims that was not included in a petition for certiorari to the Supreme Court.

Courts' Review of the Questions

The question before the *Immediato* and *Herndon* courts in this claim was whether, by requiring students to reveal to the government and fellow students where they perform charitable service, the mandatory community service programs violated the students' privacy rights guaranteed by the Ninth and Fourteenth Amendments. In answering this question the courts dealt with each aspect of the students' claim: violation of privacy of personal information and independence of decision-making; chilling of the exercise of constitutional rights; and the service program reporting requirement deserving a heightened level of review by the court. The courts rejected each part of the claim.

The courts rejected the notion that the personal information required for disclosure by a student on the school's reporting form is of the type for which students have an expectation of privacy. (See Figures 1-7, pages 55-61.) Because a student has a wide range of listed organizations to serve plus the alternative to propose an additional one, a student can choose an option that will not necessitate revealing any "deeply-held political or religious beliefs."[206] What is more, no matter which service organization is chosen, a participating student needs only to disclose the name of the organization. A student does not need to justify the choice or to affirm any agreement with that organization's purposes or activities. The student needs only to disclose what was done and what was learned from the service.

The courts found that the information disclosed does not differ significantly from information disclosed in other, traditional school assignments to which the students did not object. For example, students disclose personal choices when they write about their favorite presidents, travel experiences, books, songs, and personal heroes or models. They disclose personal information

---

[205] Herndon II, 89 F.3d at 177.
[206] Immediato II, 73 F.3d at 963.

when they select elective courses such as foreign languages or extracurricular activities such as choir, jazz band, and chess club. All such choices involve some "indicia of personal preference or opinion,"[207] but are not within the "zone of privacy" protected by the Supreme Court[208] The *Herndon* district court held, "A student's choice of projects and reaction to those projects does not reveal such intimate or personal information that would give rise to a reasonable expectation of privacy."[209] Given this situation, the disclosure required on the school questionnaires and in class discussions did not "force" the student "to reveal or suppress moral judgments"[210] and did not "implicate any constitutional privacy right or interest."[211]

The courts also held that the service programs did not violate the second type of privacy interest claimed above and derived from *Whalen*, the right to protect independence in making certain kinds of important decisions. The courts identified examples of such personal important decisions protected in Supreme Court opinions: deciding to have an abortion;[212] using contraceptives;[213] marrying inter-racially;[214] and choosing a private rather than a public school.[215] After comparing the students' decisions with the ones protected by the right of privacy, according to Supreme Court precedents, the *Herndon I* court concluded, "The right of privacy has been held to protect only significant, personal decisions. The situation Plaintiffs seek to include within the right of privacy does not fall within the sphere of such decisions."[216]

What is more, the Second Circuit appellate court considered whether a service program would be constitutional if the students did have a privacy right implicated by the questionnaire and class discussions conducted in the course Managing Your Future.[217] The court, following a precedent set in Barry, determined that the cor-

---

[207] Immediato I, 873 F.Supp. at 853.
[208] Herndon I, 99 F.Supp. at 1454, quoting Paul v. Davis, 424 U.S. 693, 96 S.Ct. 1155, 47 L.Ed.2d 405 (1996).
[209] *Id.*, citing Walls, *supra* note 207.
[210] Immediato I, 873 F.Supp. at 853.
[211] Immediato II, 73 F.3d at 463.
[212] Roe v. Wade, 410 U.S. 113, 93 S.Ct 705, 35 L.Ed.2d 147 (1973).
[213] Griswold v. Connecticut, 381 U.S. 479, 85 S.Ct. 1678, 14 L.Ed.2d 510 (1965).
[214] Loving v. Virginia, 388 U.S. 1, 87 S.Ct. 1817, 18 L.Ed.2d 1010 (1967).
[215] Pierce, 268 U.S. 510.
[216] Herndon I, 899 F.Supp. at 1455.
[217] Managing Your Future is a 10-week required course conducted for seniors in Rye Neck High School by guidance counselors. The service program is part of this course.

rect level of review for a compelled disclosure of personal information is an "intermediate balancing approach."[218] This intermediate approach met the request of the plaintiffs, set forth in their complaint and briefs, that some form of heightened level of review be applied. The court then concluded that because the program had a definite educational purpose to further the state's interest in educating children and because it requires "disclosure of minimal (if any) personal information," the service program was "on balance, easily constitutional."[219]

Finally, the *Immediato* and *Herndon* courts also concluded that the service programs did not chill the plaintiffs' ability to exercise their constitutional rights. The programs' reporting requirements did not elicit disclosure of every organization served by the students. Nor did the programs in any way prohibit the students from serving non-approved organizations on their own time without obtaining credit for the service. In this way the students could avoid disclosure of personal beliefs if they felt the need to do so because the disclosure requirements only concerned the service hours needed for credit. This result was "not so profound a burden as to raise significant constitutional concerns."[220]

In short, the answer to the question posed by the plaintiffs was NO. The courts rejected the students' claim in every aspect, including the court precedents brought to support the claims made. The courts found no support for the notion that the students' Fourteenth Amendment rights to privacy prohibit the school from requiring the students to disclose the organizations for which they performed a limited service in conjunction with a reasonable educational requirement.[221]

---

[218] Immediato II, 73 F.3d at 463.
[219] *Id.*
[220] *Id.*
[221] *Id.* at 464.

AGENCY EXPERIENCE SUMMARY FORM

(To be completed for each different Community Service activity)

Name _____ School _____ Grade Level ____

Please Provide the following information about your Community Service Experience. You may use a plain sheet of paper for additional information if needed.

1. Where did you complete this service? How many hours did you serve?

2. What were your duties?

3. How did these duties relate to the mission of the organization?

4. What did you gain from this experience?

5. How are you contributing to the community by completing this service?

_____

Signature   Date

Please return to your counselor to be attached to your Student Record Card

---

Figure 1. Bethlehem High School's Agency Experience Summary Form
(Plaintiffs argued the information required in this and the following six forms, violated the students' rights to privacy.)

Attached is the Community Service application form. Please follow the checklist below.

1. Complete the entire application.
2. Obtain ALL signatures before starting hours.
3. Begin service hours and start keeping your journal — see example below.
4. Complete hours and journal.
5. Have your journal read and signed by a teacher or your guidance counselor.
6. Turn in your time card and your journal to your guidance counselor for credit.

Journal example: (typed facsimile)

Dec. 5. *SPCA-* *Walked 3 dogs* *groomed 6 cats* *helped admit 5 kittens* *fed and watered animals*	*Animals really enjoy being cared for — they like people! I felt bad about the kittens — they need homes. I hope we get people to adopt them.*
Dec. 12 *Helped with animal adoptions*	*It was great to see so many pets get homes. I hope they are all treated well. Some people were not very patient having to wait because we were so busy.*
Dec. 19 *Watch the Vet give shots and try to save a litter of puppies found along the road. Two of them died.* *Answered phone calls —* *gave information about animal adoption.*	*It was really sad to see the puppies and know that some people are so cruel. I wish they had just brought them to the SPCA if they didn't want them. Maybe they didn't know that we'd take them and care for them.*

Figure 2. Bethlehem High School's Double-Entry Journal Example

---

RYE NECK HIGH SCHOOL
1992 - 1993

COMMUNITY SERVICE HOURS

Student Name: _____

Date	Hours	Place	Type of Service
_____	_____	_____	_____
_____	_____	_____	_____
_____	_____	_____	_____
_____	_____	_____	_____
_____	_____	_____	_____
_____	_____	_____	_____

(Please use second sheet if more room is needed)

Advisor Signature (Pre-Approval) _____

Student Signature _____

Advisor Signature (on completion) _____

Contact _____

Telephone _____

Comments _____

Figure 3. Rye Neck High School's Community Service Hours Form

NAME:_____

SUMMARIZE YOUR COMMUNITY SERVICE
(WHERE, WHEN, WHAT DID YOU DO)

_____
_____
_____
_____
_____
_____

WHAT DID YOU GAIN FROM THIS SERVICE

_____
_____
_____
_____
_____
_____

ANY CAREER CONNECTION

_____
_____
_____
_____
_____
_____

FURTHER COMMENTS

Figure 4. Rye Neck High School's Reporting and Reflecting Form

CHAPEL HILL HIGH SCHOOL
SERVICE LEARNING PROGRAM
SERVICE AGENCY SIGN-IN SHEET

Name of Agency: _____ Phone: _____

Name of Student	Type Activity	#Hours	Verified By	Date
1.				
2.				
3.				
4.				
5.				
6.				
7.				
8.				
9.				
10.				
11.				
12.				
13.				
14.				
15.				
16.				
17.				
18.				
19.				
20.				

Signature of Agency Representative: _____

Date: _____

Figure 5. Chapel Hill's Service Agency Sign-in Sheet

TO BE COMPLETED BY THE STUDENT AFTER EACH SERVICE-LEARNING ACTIVITY:

SERVICE LEARNING PROGRAM
STUDENT SERVICE RECORD

Name _____ Class _____

Name of Site   #of Hours   Date Performed   Verified By
_____   _____   _____   _____

Briefly describe your duties and any special feelings or memories you have from this experience:

_____
_____
_____
_____
_____
_____
_____
_____
_____
_____

Name of Site   #of Hours   Date Performed   Verified By
_____   _____   _____   _____

Briefly describe your duties and any special feelings or memories you have from this experience:

_____
_____
_____
_____
_____
_____
_____
_____

Figure 6. Chapel Hill's Student Service Record

Chapel Hill High School
Service-Learning Program
Experience Summary Form

AT THE COMPLETION OF YOUR 50 HOURS OF SERVICE-LEARNING, CHOOSE ONE SITE WHERE YOU PERFORMED YOUR VOLUNTEER SERVICE AND REFLECT ON YOUR EXPERIENCES IN A 1-2 PAGE PAPER. THE FOLLOWING QUESTIONS MAY BE USED AS GUIDELINES OR IDEAS FOR DISCUSSION.

1) How have you changed/grown from your service-learning experience? (e.g., changes in attitudes, changes in actions toward others, changes in feelings about self, new career interests, etc.). What kind of new skills have you learned?

2) What did you contribute? What did other people learn from you?

3) What were your first impressions of the people served? Have those first impressions changed any? What did you learn about the people you helped?

4) Were you surprised by anything that took place or do you have a special memory or a funny story to tell?

5) Can you suggest changes regarding your placement experience that would help the agency serve clients better?

6) What tips/suggestions could you offer new volunteers doing this type of service?

7) What happened that made you feel you would (or would not) like to do this as a career?

8) What do you see is the value of doing community service?

9) Will you continue to perform volunteer service in the future?

Figure 7. Chapel Hill's Experience Reflection Form

Mandated Community Service: Litigation Score Card

Plaintiff Claims••

		Students				Parents
		1st. A. Express Belief	13th A. Invol. Servit.	14th A. Personal Liberty	14th A. Privacy	14th A. Parental Liberty
Steirer v. Bethlehem	Dist. Ct.	B	B			
	3rd Cir. App.	B	B, A			
	Petit. Cert**	B	B			
Immediato v. Rye Neck	Dist. Ct.		B	B	B	B
	2nd Cir. App.		B	B	B	B
	Petit. Cert**			B		B
Herndon v. Chapel Hill	Dist. Ct.		B	B	B	B
	4th Cir. App.		B, F	B		B
	Petit. Cert**			B		B

•• = District & appellate courts rejected all plaintiffs' claims
** = Supreme Court denied certiorari
A = Alternate analysis used in affirming district court decision
B = Brought by plaintiff
F = Flawed reasoning by dist. ct., but app.ct. with other reasoning
affirmed dist. ct. decision.

Figure 8. Litigation Score Card

Chapter IV: Commentary on the Court Cases

The concept of community service by high school students is not new. Schools have been mandating community service since the early 1990s. In 1983 Ernest Boyer in *High School* called for community service as a way to reform education. Other educational reformers, including John Dewey and his disciples, have been calling for a reconnection of schools with society via community-based learning projects since early this century.

What is new is the growth of required community service, either integrated into course work or existing as an add-on to the core of the high school curriculum. The three legal actions challenging mandatory community service in Federal Court alleged violations of the constitutional rights of parents and students. While these three lawsuits are over now, the issues raised by them still deserve close attention not only for historical insight but also as clues to some of the current political action as well as the direction that future lawsuits may well take.

The Role of the Lower Federal Courts

From a legal perspective the results of the lawsuits are not so surprising, given the Supreme Court precedents concerning the First, Thirteenth, and Fourteenth Amendments to the Constitution. The federal district and appellate courts had little leeway in deciding as they did despite the criticisms[222] that several law students have made in their articles on mandated community service,

---

[222] Much of the criticism by the law students deals with making community service mandatory. Yet none of these critic students complained about making school attendance mandatory or making two years of mathematics or history, for example, a graduation requirement.

mainly on the Steirer decisions in the Third Circuit.[223] After all, the role of the lower courts is to apply the precedents that the Supreme Court establishes, not to make new law through their own interpretation of the Constitution. It is for this reason that the Second Circuit *Immediato* court explicitly refused to "break new ground" regarding Fourteenth Amendment parental rights and "decline(d) plaintiffs' invitation" to be the first court to expand the students' Fourteenth Amendment personal liberty rights.[224]

The lower courts performed according to role even without announcing that they refused to break new ground. For example, in regard to the plaintiffs' request for an opt-out provision the *Immediato I* district court dealt with the issue summarily, explaining that there is no federal case law precedent on an opt-out provision in an educational curriculum matter.[225] The *Immediato II* appellate court only alluded to the opt-out request, denying the request by rejecting the underlying issue that distinguished between exposure and action. The two *Herndon* courts were silent on the opt-out claim that had no precedent.

---

[223] *See* Bruce J. Rome, Note, Mandatory Community Service in Public High Schools, 28 U.S.F. L. Rev. 517 (1994), claiming that community service is "a form of self-expression" and that under a "traditional analysis" it violates the Thirteenth Amendment (at 548, 560); Charters, Volunteer Work Assumes a New Role in Public High school, 23 J. Law & Educ. 607 (1994), concluding that the Steirer decision "will remain law for the time being an unfortunate situation, given the appellate court's perfunctory analysis of the issues and excessive deference to the school district (at 611); and Bradley H. Kreshek, Comment, Students or Serfs? Is Mandatory Community Service a Violation of the Thirteenth Amendment?; 30 Loy. L.A. L. Rev. 809, arguing the mandatory community service "is obnoxious and repulsive to the spirit of the Thirteenth amendment and its prohibition against involuntary servitude" (at 839). On the other hand see Scott D. Minden, Note, The Constitutionality of Mandatory Community Service Programs in Public Schools, 68 S. Cal. L. Rev. 1391 (1995), concluding that the mandatory community service programs do not violate the First and Thirteenth Amendments "because these programs serve legitimate goals" and "are not merely a means of extracting free student labor for the benefit of others" (at 1393). See also Cynthia L. Brennan, Comment, Mandatory Community Service as a High School Graduation Requirement, 11 T.M. Cooley L. Rev. 253 (1994), accepting the courts' decision but questioning the wisdom of boards of education that made community service mandatory (at 276). For the view of a recent law school graduate with a subsequent doctorate in social psychology see Mark S. Sobus, Mandating Community Service: Psychological Implications of Requiring Prosocial Behavior, 19 Law & Psychol. Rev. 153 (1995), concluding that from "the psychological perspective, requiring community service of high school students is not a wise policy" and that such a policy "is unlikely to foster long-term prosocial attitudes. In fact, a coercive policy should be expected to undermine positive attributions, stifle feelings of self-determination, and ultimately make self-generated acts of community service more scarce" at (181-82).

[224] Immediato II, 73 F.3d at 461 and 463.

[225] Immediato I, 873 F. Supp. at 852.

All of the reactions by the *Immediato* and *Herndon* courts were role appropriate, given the Supreme Court's earlier directions concerning caution regarding substantive due process. These reactions to student issues were also appropriate given the generally poor record of student plaintiffs beginning in 1985 in such key cases as *New Jersey v. T.L.O.*,[226] *Bethel School Dist. v. Fraser*,[227] *Hazelwood School Dist. v. Kuhlmeier*,[228] and *Vernonia School Dist. v. Acton*,[229] concerning search and seizure protection and free speech.[230] In large measure, this point explains why the reasoning and conclusions of courts in three circuits were so similar.

On the other hand, it is incorrect to think that the courts had no leeway at all and could not have found a legitimate point on which to support the plaintiffs if they had wanted to. Three possibilities for leeway follow. First, in regard to expressive behavior under the First Amendment, it is certainly possible to have found that mandatory community service does constitute expressive speech according to the two-prong *Spence* test.[231] Just as it is possible to infer that students standing silently at attention agree with the flag salute and believe the words of the pledge of allegiance to the American flag and the republic for which it stands, so is it possible to infer that a student performing community service at the American Red Cross blood drive believes in the value of donating blood that underpins the service activity. Such an inference is especially true when the service program is new and community people are not familiar with the requirement of service.

What is more, the Third Circuit did have precedents to follow if it needed them to reach a conclusion that community service is an expressive activity. In *Lipp v. Morris*,[232] a 1978 case dealing with an objection to standing during the flag salute, the Third Circuit appellate court held that "mere standing" was unconstitutional. It cited a case from the Fifth Circuit[233] and a case from the Second Circuit[234] as being "precisely on point" and then quoted the dis-

---

[226] 469 U.S. 325, 105 S.Ct. 733, 83 L.Ed.2d 720 (1985).

[227] 478 U.S. 675.

[228] 484 U.S. 260, 108 S.Ct. 562, 98 L.Ed.2d 592 (1988).

[229] 515 U.S. 646, 115 S.Ct. 2386, 132 L.Ed.2d 564 (1995).

[230] The student plaintiff did win the graduation prayer case, Lee v. Weisman, 505 U.S. 577, 112 S.Ct. 2649, 120 L.Ed.2d 467 (1992).

[231] 418 U.S. at 410-411.

[232] 579 F.2d 834 (3rd Cir. 1978).

[233] Banks v. Board of Public Instruction, 450 F.2d 1103 (5th Cir. 1971).

[234] Goetz v. Ansell, 477 F.2d 636 (2nd Cir. 1973).

trict court judge: "This mandatory condition upon the student's right not to participate in the flag salute ceremony is an unconstitutional requirement that the student engage in a form of speech and may not be enforced."[235] The Third Circuit also had the Supreme Court's precedent in *Barnette*,[236] dealing with reciting the pledge of allegiance, where the Court held that refusal to say the pledge is an expressive act as is the saying of the Pledge.

Thus, the Third Circuit could probably have rationalized, following its own decision in *Lipp* and the Supreme Court in *Barnette*, a decision to sustain Steirer's First Amendment claim. It did have some leeway not to conclude that "the Program does not compel expression protected by the First Amendment...."[237]

Second, the courts probably could have found a way to support the parents in their Fourteenth Amendment claim. Parents have the primary responsibility for their child's upbringing, and the court could have deferred to them when the clash arose regarding off-campus service. After all, the parents did not question matters related to in-school behavior but felt that in a conflict about off-campus service, not performed under the direct supervision of the school and not integrated into the curriculum core, the balance should shift in favor of their belief and their child's belief in individual conscience instead of the government's concern about citizenship.

The courts could have given considerable weight, if they had wanted to, to the fact that the student plaintiffs showed their faith in public education and citizenship by attending public high schools and by accepting the in-school requirement to learn citizenship values in the required academic courses. The students were willing to accept the courts' ruling that a school district may institute a mandatory community service program. In addition, the plaintiff parents sought only an "opt-out remedy" to "preserve their parental liberty right," arguing in an allusion to *Tinker* [238] that an opt-out provision "would not lead to the disruption of classes, interfere with the instruction of other students, or cause any other administrative difficulty."[239] Given the circumstances of

---

[235] Lipp, 579 F.2d at 836. The New Jersey statute under consideration, N.J. Stat. Ann. § 18A:36-3, required, in pertinent part, that in saluting the flag students "show full respect to the flag while the pledge is being given merely by standing at attention, boys removing the headdress."

[236] 319 U.S. 624.

[237] Steirer II, 987 F.2d at 997.

[238] 393 U.S. 503.

[239] Immediato's Reply Brief to the Second Circuit Court of Appeals at 7.

the service program and a then-recent New York State court decision supporting parents' objection to the distribution of condoms
in high school based on parental rights,[240] the court probably could
have rationalized supporting the parental liberty right, at least to
agree to the request to opt out of community service in light of the
good faith behavior by the plaintiffs when in school.

Finally, in regard to the students' Fourteenth Amendment privacy right, it is certainly possible to have found that in high school
students are under considerable peer pressure and that the revealing of personal information threatens the students' sense of privacy.
While there was no pressure in the challenged programs from
teachers and administrators to reveal more on paper than the answers to the questions asked on the reporting form, pressure from
teachers and students could well have existed in a free-flowing
class or homeroom discussion.

The Supreme Court has recognized that peer pressure exists.
In *Lee v. Weisman,* a case dealing with prayer at a high school graduation ceremony, the Court recognized that peer pressure, "though
subtle and indirect, can be as real as any overt compulsion....
Research in psychology supports the common assumption that
adolescents are often susceptible to pressure from their peers towards conformity, and that the influence is strongest in matters of
social convention."[241] The courts had the leeway to conclude that
a similar peer pressure might invade a student's privacy and cause
that student to conform during a class discussion in which participants are expected to disclose personal information.

The Supreme Court and the Plaintiffs' Petitions for Review

In any case, even if the judges had more leeway in the lower
courts than they wanted to acknowledge, including the leeway to
be bold enough to break new ground regarding the substantive
component of the Due Process Clause, the probability was high
that the courts would defer to the accepted power of a local board
of education to determine the curriculum of its schools. What is
more, once the decisions were made by the district and appellate

---

[240] Alfonso, 606 N.Y.S. 2D 259
[241] 505 U.S. at 593.

courts, the probability was also high, strictly from a quantitative perspective, that the Supreme Court would deny certiorari to the plaintiffs' petitions. By the time the petition from *Herndon* was filed the probability of denial of certiorari was even higher because there was no qualitative split existing among the Third, Second, and Fourth Circuits regarding all the claims opposing mandatory community service.

The Supreme Court knew early on that there was no split among the circuits, including the First Circuit, on the key issue of parental rights in curricular matters.[242] In the First Circuit, a recent case concerned compulsory student attendance at a sexually explicit awareness assembly in a public high school that dealt with Acquired Immune Deficiency Syndrome (AIDS). In *Brown v. Hot, Sexy, and Safer Productions*[243] the plaintiff parents claimed that the high school violated their right to direct the upbringing and education of the children. They cited the precedents of *Meyer* and *Pierce* just as the parents in *Immediato* and *Herndon* did.

The First Circuit held that parents do not have a "fundamental constitutional right to dictate the curriculum of the public school to which they have chosen to send their children."[244] Distinguishing the case at bar from *Meyer* and *Pierce*, respectively, the court stated that "it is fundamentally different for the state to say to a parent, 'you can't teach your child German or send him to a parochial school,' than for the parent to say to the state, 'you can't teach my child subjects that are morally offensive to me.'"[245] The First Circuit rejected the parents' claim, believing that it would have required schools to "cater a curriculum" for each individual student and would have caused too great a burden on the public educational system.[246] A key reason appeared to lie in the choice available to parents. The court appeared to be saying what the *Steirer, Immediato*, and *Herndon* courts said in regard to the involuntary servitude claim as well as the parental rights claim: once parents have chosen the public schools, the parents' rights (and

---

[242] On January 2, 1996 the Second Circuit issued its Immediato decision. On March 4, 1996 the Supreme Court denied certiorari to the Brown petitioners. On May 15, the Immediatos petitioned for certiorari. On July 11, 1996 the Fourth Circuit issued its Herndon decision and denied a rehearing in banc on August 28, 1996. On October 7, 1996 the Supreme Court denied certiorari to the Immediatos and to the Reinhards on February 18, 1997.

[243] 68 F.3d 525 (1st Cir. 1995), *cert. denied*, 516 U.S. 1159, 134 L.Ed. 2d 191,116 S.Ct. 1044 (1996).

[244] *Id.* at 533.

[245] *Id.* at 534.

[246] *Id.*

the students' rights) are limited by the interests of the state in the education of children and the operation of the schools.

Even more recently, in a case that was decided after the petitions of *Steirer, Immediato,* and *Reinhard*[247] were not granted certiorari by the Supreme Court, the Tenth Circuit also held against parents who claimed their parental rights to direct the upbringing and education of their children. In *Swanson v. Guthrie Independent School District #I-L,*[248] the Swansons wished to enroll their home-schooled daughter in selected eighth-grade classes in the Guthrie school. The school district refused to permit the girl to attend on a part-time basis and to "pick and choose which courses" to take.[249] The court held that decisions about allocation of scarce resources (there was no state funding for part timers) "as well as what curriculum to offer or require, are uniquely committed to the discretion of local school authorities...."[250] The court rejected the claimed right of the parents to "override the local school board's explicit decision" on attendance.[251]

The Tenth Circuit Court of Appeals, while accepting the general right of parents to direct their children's education, as decided in *Pierce*, referred to recent cases (among them *Immediato*) that "have made it clear that this constitutional right is limited in scope."[252] The court held that the parental right to direct a child's education does not have the reach claimed by the parents, saying that "parents simply do not have a constitutional right to control each and every aspect of their children's education and oust the state's authority over that subject."[253] In addition, the Tenth Circuit rejected the parents' request that the court apply a strict scrutiny test to the board of education's policy on attendance. Rather than require the school district to show a compelling interest for implementing its full-time-or-nothing attendance policy, the court used a reasonable-means test because the attendance policy was deemed neutral in character and of general application.[254] Thus, there was no split among the First, Second, Third,

---

[247] The petition for certiorari in Herndon was filed under the name of the Reinhard family because the Herndon family moved outside of the school district for reasons unrelated to the litigation. The Reinhards, with the Herndons, were the plaintiffs in the lower court proceedings.

[248] 135 F.3d 694 (10th Cir. 1998).

[249] *Id.* at 700.

[250] *Id.*

[251] *Id.*

[252] *Id.* at 699.

[253] *Id.*

[254] *Id.* at 698.

and Fourth Circuits before the Supreme Court denied certiorari to *Immediato* and *Reinhard*, and subsequently there is also no split with the Tenth Circuit in regard to both the scope of parental rights and the level of review to apply to those rights.

The four circuits (First, Second, Fourth, and Tenth) that most recently have dealt with parental rights in matters of public school curriculum have held in favor of the schools. As the Fourth Circuit pointed out, only when plaintiffs have combined a First Amendment free exercise concern under the special conditions of *Yoder* with a Fourteenth Amendment parental rights claim has the Supreme Court held that parental rights were fundamental.[255] Because the parents in *Herndon* brought their claim on secular, not religious grounds, the Fourth Circuit rejected the claim that their right was a fundamental one, quoting a passage from *Yoder* to support its position: "A way of life, however virtuous and admirable, may not be interposed as a barrier to reasonable state regulation of education if it is based on purely secular considerations...."[256]

Significantly, the First Circuit in *Brown*, upholding the district court's dismissal of plaintiff's claim regarding a mandatory AIDS assembly, stated explicitly that even if the parental right were fundamental (a critical claim in *Immediato* and *Herndon*, as well), "we find that...the plaintiffs have failed to demonstrate an intrusion of constitutional magnitude of this right."[257] The *Brown* court in this way signaled all parents that their claim and argument must be more than the assertion that parental rights are fundamental; that is, parents must not think that the status of their right will be enough to win their lawsuit. What parents need to do is demonstrate that their parental right outweighs the government's countervailing interest in and obligation to children and society at large. (See the following chapter on new legislation for more on the topic of parental rights.)

Despite the signal from the *Brown* decision, the logic of the Immediatos' and Reinhards' petitions for certiorari was straightforward and it reflected the strategy used by the plaintiffs during their circuit court appeals. The claims raised in these two peti-

---

[255] Herndon II, 89 F.3d at 178.

[256] *Id.*, quoting Yoder, 406 U.S. at 215. The quoted partial sentence ends with: "the very concept of ordered liberty precludes allowing every person to make his own standards on matters of conduct in which society as a whole has important interests" (at 215-216).

[257] 68 F.3d at 533.

tions involved only the Fourteenth Amendment. These were new ones for the Supreme Court regarding community service in that Steirer's earlier petition raised only the Thirteenth Amendment and First Amendment issues on which the Court had spoken many times previously. In contrast to the petition for certiorari by the Steirers, the petitions by the Immediatos and the Reinhards asked the Court to break new ground twice, once in regard to parental liberty rights and once in regard to student personal liberty.

The parental rights claim was the key one filed, and in it the families contended that they lost in the lower courts because the lower court judges applied the wrong standard for evaluating the schools' service programs. That is, the courts applied the low, relaxed rational basis standard rather than the heightened standard of strict scrutiny. The plaintiffs believed that this factor was critical in their cases, just as the *Herndon* district court had said it was: "A crucial determination in examining the constitutionality of a challenged governmental statute or regulation under the substantive component of the Due Process Clause, and on which the parties agree, is the appropriate standard of review."[258]

The families explicitly claimed that at the time of the earlier *Meyer* and *Pierce* cases, which set the precedents for their cases, only a single tier standard of review existed.[259] The families requested the Supreme Court to declare parental rights as fundamental rights. They said, "If parental rights were affirmed as fundamental, then public school programs that burdened those rights would be subject to strict scrutiny."[260]

The petitioners believed that if the Supreme Court used the correct, heightened standard now available to them, the mandatory community service programs would fail to meet the test because no compelling reason existed to override their rights. Or, at least, the parents would win the relief they were requesting: "...only to opt out of certain objectionable programs required by the public schools."[261] In short, a declaration of parental rights as fundamental ones with the consequential use of a strict scrutiny test would save the parents' cause, according to the plaintiffs in their last request to the courts. However, this approach was pre-

---

[258] Herndon I, 899 F.Supp. at 1449.
[259] Immediato's petition for a Writ of Certiorari at 9-18. *See also* Reinhard's Petition for a Writ of Certiorari at 10-20.
[260] *Id* at 21.
[261] *Id*. at 23.

cisely what the *Brown* court in the First Circuit specifically indicated was not enough to work for the plaintiffs in Massachusetts.

The student personal liberty part of the Fourteenth Amendment claim did not fare any better in the petition to the Supreme Court. As petitioners, the Immediatos and the Reinhards requested the Supreme Court to recognize an established privilege, just as they had requested the appellate courts to do. "Consequently, petitioners do not seek creation of a new constitutional right, but merely seek recognition of a privilege 'long recognized at common law as essential to the orderly pursuit of happiness by free men.'"[262] However, despite their statement that they were not requesting the creation of a new constitutional right, they were requesting something new, namely, Fourteenth Amendment protection of a person's right to refuse governmental imposition of a duty to serve his or her community.

The Supreme Court would have made a significant leap in jurisprudence to permit people to refuse to be regulated by the government because the Court's precedents are to the contrary, as already noted in the courts' treatment of the involuntary servitude claim. To permit such refusal via recognition of the claimed privilege might lead to the public refusing to fulfill jury duty, provide pro bono legal representation for people unable to afford a lawyer, perform military service directly or indirectly, study the 3Rs, comply with compulsory attendance in school, get compulsory vaccinations, pay taxes to build super highways and hire police officers, and refuse to obey traffic lights. In this regard, Rob Tier and Suzanne Goldsmith, general counsel and director of the Community Service Project, respectively, of the American Alliance for Rights and Responsibilities, wrote:

> It is a direct attack on the notion that the communities can ask anything of the individual. The same mindset that rejects a service-learning requirement is likely to reject jury duty, military duty, perhaps even the notion of highway speed limits. In all these instances, the community, speaking through its elected government, asks the individual for a small or large sacrifice of his or her time in service of the greater good.[263]

---

[262] *Id.* at 28, quoting Meyer, 262 U.S. at 399. *See also* Reinhard's Petition for a Writ of Certiorari at 25.

[263] Tier and Goldsmith, "Teaching Citizenship is Not Slavery," 16 *Education Week* 35 (May 24, 1995).

The questions, therefore, before the Supreme Court, in regard to the student personal liberty claim, as well as in regard to the involuntary servitude claim, were: What is reasonable for national, state, and local governments to require of their constituents? What degree of governmental regulation is permissible? What is the reasonable balance between governmental action for the general welfare in a democracy and an individual's liberty? How can democracy survive without calling upon people to serve their communities?

Justice Brennan, when addressing the issue of library materials in a public school, said that it is "long recognized that local school boards have broad discretion in the management of school affairs."[264] The Court has declared that there is no federal right to a public education,[265] thereby allowing each state or each state's local boards of education (i.e., people serving their communities without pay as part of their civic duty), as empowered by state law, to determine the curriculum of its public school.

Thus, the Court already had spoken on the privilege of refusing to abide by reasonable curriculum decisions made at the state or local level. The Supreme Court by its denial of certiorari indicated that it was not prepared to expand the protection afforded to students through the concept of substantive due process, which is just what the lower courts reported about the Court in their decisions. The Court also indicated that it was not prepared to upset the traditional role of home rule in American education. In sum, students may be regulated by their boards of education just as the federal and state governments may require of adults jury duty, military service, and work on building roads.

The Plaintiffs' Spin on Community Service

Part of the legal problem in these three lawsuits is the spin the plaintiffs put on the concept of community service. The plaintiffs' language is important to note because it is carefully chosen. The petitions for certiorari by the Steirers, Immediatos, and Reinhards, as well as other documents by the plaintiffs, frame the issue before the courts in terms of performing "charitable service to others."[266] To call community service "charitable service to oth-

---

[264] Pico, 457 U.S. at 863.
[265] San Antonio Ind. Sch. Dist. v. Rodriguez, 411 U.S. 1, 93 S.Ct. 1278, 36 L.Ed.2d 16 (1973).
[266] Reinhard's Petition for a Writ of Certiorari at 23.

ers" or "charitable work"[267] is a narrowing and misleading linguistic twist, especially when used often, as it was.

Some of the approved activities[268] in all three challenged programs do involve what may be called charitable organizations such as Westchester Lighthouse for the Blind, Home for the Aged, Special Olympics, and March of Dimes Birth Defects Foundation. These organizations are typical of the traditional organizations which serve people in need. However, the high school community service programs also approved civic organizations and governmental agencies that are not charities. Civic organizations and activities serve everybody, the needy as well as the comfortable and privileged in society. Such organizations provide service opportunities that are particularly important to students who philosophically object to being required to perform charitable work. This group of organizations includes, for example, the City of Marmaroneck Traffic Survey, Rescue Earth's Environmental Future, Chapel Hill Bicentennial, the Public Library, and the Community Recycling Program. When working for and serving with these organizations, some of which are governmental while others are private non-profit, students in effect help themselves as well as others.

Self-interest, along with citizenship, is furthered when students work, for example, solving a traffic problem or promoting a healthy and balanced use of natural resources. Because not all approved and participating service opportunities in Bethlehem, Rye Neck, and Chapel Hill high schools were charitable ones, the plaintiff students did not need to perform charitable service; these students could have performed civic service.

It was not only the plaintiffs who did not make the important distinction between charitable service to the needy and civic service to everyone. In the material sent to students in June 1993 by the coordinators of the Rye Neck High School program, the following appears:

What counts as service?
The direct provision of basic human service to a person or people in need without remuneration. A minimum of half of your service must be performed outside of school. You may work *with people in need—people who are poor, homeless,*

---

[267] Immediato's Petition for a Writ of Certiorari at 25.
[268] For a list of Chapel Hill High School's approved activities see the Appendix to Herndon I, 899 F.Supp. at 1456.

*handicapped, or in need of education, supervisor, or companion-
ship. Activities such as clerical work, aiding, coaching a sport
do not qualify.*[269] [emphasis in the original]

Apparently even the Rye Neck coordinators originally had a
narrow and mistaken concept of what constituted community service. In practice, the Rye Neck program never was so narrow.
Although the official legal response by the Rye Neck school district to Immediato's interrogatories (submitted to the plaintiffs and
the Southern New York District Court in July, 1994) was different
and broader,[270] the plaintiffs and the Association for Objective Law,
as amicus curiae, exploited the language of the earlier handout to
students when they described and referred to the program in their
briefs. Perhaps it was this very conceptual confusion and error
that led the Fourth Circuit judges to accept their plaintiffs' rhe-
torical twist of language and to say, "Freedom from compulsory
charitable service is not among the rights the [Supreme] Court
has recognized, and the Court has expressed forcefully that we
should expand the sphere of rights only with great caution."[271]

Other aspects of the language that was used also set a misleading context. In his petition for certiorari *Reinhard* used the
expression mandatory volunteering. In claiming that "charitable
service" to people in need "must come from an individual's conscience," he stated, "That is why the colloquial expression for the
school district's program—'mandatory volunteering'—sounds so
strange, so oxymoronic."[272] Later he referred again to the "school
district's 'mandatory volunteering' program" as contradictory to
"this Nation's history of voluntarism."[273] The spin here poked

---

[269] *See* Joint Appendix for Immediato II, *supra* note 4, at 54. It is important to note that
this quoted section no longer appears in the June 1996 material distributed to students.
[270] The official response states that the purpose of the service program is "to have
students learn about the community and the needs of the community, to learn what
services are necessary to meet the needs of the community and its citizens, to meet
people and see what they do, and, if possible, to become involved in internships with
government officials and agencies." (p.2). This statement of purposes was incorporated
into the Joint Statement of Material Facts submitted to the Immediato District Court at
6. This language is in stark contrast to the language of the two coordinators of the
program, as quoted above. Nevertheless, Immediato in his brief to the District Court
used the language of the coordinators, which was favorable to his narrow view, rather
than the language of the school district, which offers a broader definition of community
service. All are reproduced in the Joint Appendix submitted to the Second Circuit
Court of Appeals for purposes of Immediato II.
[271] Herndon II, 87 F.3d at 179.
[272] Reinhard's Petition for a Writ of Certiorari at 23.
[273] *Id.* at 24.

fun at the Chapel Hill program and was misleading rhetoric. The challenged high schools never claimed that their students were volunteering for community service any more than students volunteered to take courses in English in the 9th grade or volunteered to attend school in the first place. These schools required community service just as they required science and mathematics courses for graduation and just as state law required school attendance. The term mandatory volunteering served the purpose of painting an image of the service program as illogical and strange.

Another example is the use of the term force to describe the requirement of community service. Force has a connotation of physical coercion, compulsion, and power. Force has a different feel from require. In their petition for certiorari regarding their First Amendment free speech claim, the Steirer and Moralis families stated that they "believe that a state authority cannot force participation in a program that the state perceives to be in the community's interest."[274] In the next paragraph they claimed that there was "forced affirmance of the value of community service" and that "forced devotion of one's labor to the ideal of community service" is a violation of the First Amendment.[275] Such language is polemical and misleading about what all the challenged programs did: required community service but honored the students' decisions not to participate; they did not force students to participate or to affirm anything the students did not believe. Lynn Ann Steirer and David Stephen Moralis decided not to participate in their school's required community service program. Therefore, they did not meet their school district's requirement for graduation and did not graduate from their high school.

In their briefs to their respective Second and Fourth Circuit appellate courts, the students and parents stated that the "right of parents to direct and control the upbringing and education of their children is firmly established in our constitutional heritage."[276]

Their statement is not a quotation from *Pierce* but a modification of key language in *Pierce*: "...we think it entirely plain that the Act of 1922 [requiring students to attend public schools] un-

---

[274] Steirer's Petition for a Writ of Certiorari at 11.

[275] *Id.* at 12.

[276] Immediato's Brief to the Second Circuit Court of Appeals at 6 and Herndon's Brief to the Fourth Circuit Court of Appeals at 7, citing Meyer and Pierce among others. The students repeated their statement in their petitions to the Supreme Court, at 9 and 10, respectively.

reasonably interferes with the liberty of parents and guardians to *direct the upbringing and education of children under their control.*"[277] (emphasis added). Thus, the strong and repeated language of the parents, which relocated the word control from the end of the sentence so it could function as a supplemental verb for the word direct, said something different to the reader than what the Supreme Court actually said. That is, "to direct the upbringing and education ...." is not the same as "to direct and control the upbringing and education...."

Whatever the claimed purpose or the intended implications of the parents' choice of language, it is a legal and social fact that the government does have a legitimate stake in the upbringing and education of all children. The government has the right to impose regulations on parents in that regard. In fact, the parents acknowledged that the state has an interest in their children's education. "The parents also acknowledge the basic legitimacy of the district's interest in teaching students the value of service and that the service requirement is rationally related to that interest."[278]

The Supreme Court in *Yoder* said, "There is no doubt as to the power of a State, having a high responsibility for education of its citizens, to impose reasonable regulation for the control and duration of basic education."[279] The question, then, is how to balance the two legitimate concerns about the upbringing of children. Judge Brieant of the Southern New York District Court, the first judge to hear the parental liberty claim in regard to a community service program, noted this point in *Immediato I*, saying, "The issue, therefore, is whether the Program has a reasonable relation within the competency of the state."[280] In this way the judge rightly kept his eyes on the pertinent law, not the proffered rhetoric.

---

[277] Pierce, 268 U.S. at 534-35.
[278] Herndon II, 879 F.3d at 179.
[279] Yoder, 406 U.S. At 213.
[280] Immediato I, 873 F.Supp. at 852.

A Tactic of the Defendants and the Plaintiffs' Reaction to It

In describing the purpose of their community service programs to the courts all three boards of education stated that the main beneficiary of community service are the participating students. All three focused directly on the students, not the recipient individuals, recipient organizations, the schools, or the students' parents. This was a winning legal tactic. The Third Circuit accepted the Bethlehem board's position by concluding, "The record amply supports the defendants' claim that the community service program is primarily designed for the students' own benefit and education, notwithstanding some incidental benefit to the recipients of the services."[281] The Second and Fourth Circuits agreed. Nevertheless, even though the students are the primary beneficiaries of their own service, other motivations for and benefits from community service program do exist that are not merely "incidental" to the schools, the community recipients, or the parents. What is tactically sound in court for lawyers does not necessarily indicate the reality outside the courtroom door.

The plaintiff students and parents did not challenge the schools on their tactical point about purpose. Nor did they seek to change the community service programs in any way other than removal of the requirement of participation. Nor did they challenge the schools on the weaknesses of the programs as they might have by focusing on the fact that the students' service activities were not integrated into their academic curriculums. If they had challenged the service programs substantively, they could have created strong doubts in the minds of the judges as to whether these service programs, "as applied,"[282] met the rational basis standard of review because the proffered purposes were not being met.

Such a move by the plaintiff would have required an entirely different strategy in litigation, an attack on the rational basis of the programs rather than a concession to it. However, the plaintiffs did concede a loss, as shown by the Immediatos' late admission in their petition for certiorari. "Any public school requirement, no matter how onerous and invasive of parental rights and pre-

---

[281] Steirer II, 987 F.2d at 1000.
[282] Immediato I, 873 F.Supp. at 850.

rogative, could be justified as furthering some 'rational' educational objective."[283] The plaintiff families could have objected to more than just the requirement of participation had they examined the conceptual limitations of the programs, the lack of teacher-guided in-class reflection, and the further fragmentation of the curriculum.

Had the plaintiff families argued against the rational basis of their respective programs they could have at least shown publicly the weaknesses of the programs and the need for changes. They could have pointed out, for example, that the programs "as applied" were in actuality limited conceptually to a personal development focus; did not integrate community service into the students' ongoing academic courses; did not provide structured academic guidance to learn and practice the intellectual skills claimed for the programs; did not provide any evidence that the service programs had "improve[d] the students' ego and moral development" nor any evidence that they had "promote[d] higher level thinking skills such as open-mindedness";[284] and did not provide opportunity for students to reflect on their experiences under the guidance of teachers able to discuss with students the responsibilities of citizens in a democratic society.

The plaintiffs could have shown that Ernest Boyer, who in 1983 proposed the community service requirement and the new Carnegie unit,[285] had expanded his position in 1990, and that the schools failed to follow him. Boyer wrote about civic education in general and community service as one specific element of that. In looking at community service projects he called for more than a focus on the personal development purpose. He emphasized the need for a stronger intellectual purpose and called for more reflection about the service activity. He wrote:

> While such [service] projects can generate within students a sense of worth, they must be viewed as part of the educational experience and *not just an after school activity* [emphasis added]. Specifically, service projects should include evaluation by the student, linking community activity to classroom theory.

---

[283] Immediato's Petition for a Writ of Certiorari at 19.
[284] *See* Steirer I, 789 F.Supp. at 1339 for these two examples of purposes given by the Bethlehem school district.
[285] Boyer, *High School.*

I'm suggesting that civic education, by its very nature, means helping students confront social and ethical concerns and apply what they have learned. We must help them understand that not all choices—in thought and action—are equally valid. Such an education does not dictate solutions or suggest that there are simple answers for every complicated question. Rather it means helping students develop responsible ways of thinking, believing, and acting.[286]

The plaintiffs, in short, could have shown that community service was in essence just an after school activity and not integrated into the curriculum so as to achieve its intellectual and civic education purposes. Although the plaintiffs might still have lost their legal case under the rational basis standard, more cogent arguments by them about the substance of their schools' service programs rather than their virtually exclusive emphasis on the appropriate standard of review, could have led their schools to improve the design of their service programs.

Furthermore, such substantive arguments about the service programs might have prompted the judges to comment on community service in a positive vein. For example, Judge Brieant might have felt disposed to go beyond his negative remark and to comment on the wisdom and utility of the service program being challenged. He might have said more than, "Nor are we concerned with the wisdom or utility of the Program, which may seem to some to have Orwellian overtones, or be less useful to the graduates than a foundation course in Latin or English grammar."[287] Brieant and the other judges might have been encouraged to exhort the schools to strengthen their programs, that is, to bring the practice of a community service program more in line with the theory of a high quality community service program.[288] (See Chapter 7 infra.) Chief Justice Warren's opinion in *Brown v. Board of Education of Topeka*[289] is a valuable precedent for comments on the importance of a high quality public school curriculum.

---

[286] Boyer, Civic Education for Responsible Citizens, 48 Educational Leadership 7 (Nov. 1990).

[287] Immediato I, 873 F.Supp. at 850.

[288] Judge Huyett in Steirer I, 789 F.Supp. at 1339 and Judge Sloviter in Steirer II, 987 F.2d at 992, n. 2 both noted that Bethlehem's program did not include a component, as initially proposed, that would deal with teaching and training of decision making, problem, solving, and stress management skills. Nevertheless, the judges said nothing further on this matter.

[289] 347 U.S. 483.

The Plaintiffs' Reliance on a Tactic From *Mozert*

The *Immediato* plaintiffs specifically requested the court to grant them the ability to opt out of their school's community service program, thus following the tactic used by the plaintiffs in *Mozert*.[290] However, as stated earlier, the courts rejected that request. The rejection was not surprising even though the court had some leeway to do otherwise. What was surprising was the brevity of the court's response to that specific request and the reliance of the plaintiffs on *Mozert*. According to the plaintiffs, the *Mozert* court offered a hint as to what might constitute a constitutional violation regarding the required textbooks for teaching students to read. The plaintiffs stated, "...the *Mozert* court held that '[p]roof that an objecting student was required to participate beyond reading and discussing assigned materials' would raise constitutional concerns 'because the element of compulsion would then be present.'"[291]

However, the *Mozert* court was not talking simply about raising constitutional concerns, as the plaintiffs put it. The *Mozert* court was not talking about a general context dealing with free speech or secular values that is the basis of the lawsuits on mandatory community service. On the contrary, the *Mozert* court specifically referred to the Free Exercise Clause of the First Amendment, which was the basis of Mozert's claim against the school's reading series. This specification was omitted by the plaintiffs in their briefs because of their incomplete quotation from the *Mozert* decision. The complete sentence of the *Mozert* appellate decision was: "Proof that an objecting student was required to participate beyond reading and discussing assigned materials, or was disciplined for disputing assigned materials, might well implicate the Free Exercise Clause because the element of compulsion would then be present."[292] The significant omissions in the plaintiffs' quotation from *Mozert* and the rephrasing done by the plaintiffs are

---

[290] 827 F. 2d 1058.
[291] Herndon's Brief to the Sixth Circuit Court of Appeals 17.
[292] 825 F.2d at 1064.

an indication that the plaintiffs had no support for their position from *Mozert*, which dealt with Free Exercise matters under the First Amendment.[293]

In addition, the *Mozert* court unanimously ruled against an opt-out provision for a curricular matter. In other words, the *Mozert* court also deferred to an educational policy decision made by a local board of education. *Mozert* respected the power and authority of the local board of education to decide curriculum matters. In his concurring opinion in *Mozert*, Judge Boggs specifically phrased the issue in terms disadvantageous to the community service plaintiffs. Judge Boggs's words with only a slight variation could well have appeared in *Steirer, Immediato,* or *Herndon*:

> Preliminarily, as my colleagues indicate, we make no judgment on the educational, political, or social soundness of the school board's decision to adopt this particular set of books and this general curricular approach. This is not a case about fundamentalist Christians or any particular set of beliefs. It is about the constitutional limits on the powers of school boards to prescribe a curriculum....As we ultimately decide here, on the present state of constitutional law, the school board is entitled to say, "my way or the highway....[O]ur mandate is limited to carrying out the commands of the Constitution and the Supreme Court."[294]

Therefore, it seems strange that the plaintiffs rested their claim for an opt-out provision on a decision that decisively ruled against the *Mozert* plaintiffs and, by analogy, the community service plaintiffs, by analogy. It seems that the *Mozert* decision is more appropriately a case for the defendants to quote than the plaintiffs.

---

[293] For a parallel situation in a case that was published after the above text was written, see Boring v. Buncombe County Board of Education, 136 F.3d 364, 373 (4th Cir. 1998) where Judge Luttig showed the weakness of the dissenting opinion. (Boring dealt with a First Amendment claim that a teacher had a right to participate in the making up of the curriculum.) Judge Luttig stated, "From its perceived need to omit from the Hazelwood passages upon which it explicitly relies and partially quotes, all references within those passages — even within the holding itself— to the fact that the Court was concerned in that case only with student speech, it is clear that Hazelwood offers no support for its [the dissent's] position in this case."

[294] Mozert, 827 F. 2d at 1073, 1074, 1081.

Future Possible Changes by and For the Plaintiffs

The plaintiffs lost their challenges in three significant lawsuits. As a result, the legal challenge to mandatory community service now appears to be over unless dissatisfied students, parents, and their lawyers approach their situations differently. The legal organization that has backed the plaintiffs so far, The Institute for Justice, realizes this conclusion and will allocate further resources and time to challenge community service only if one or more external and/or internal changes occur.

One internal change might be a shift by lawyers to use a case that combines claims of violation of the free speech and the religion clauses of the First Amendment with claims based on the substantive due process rights of the Fourteenth Amendment. The reasoning is to strengthen the opposition to mandatory community service by connecting it to precedents that protect fundamental religious beliefs, free speech, and parental rights. Of course, the lawyers must wait for or solicit such a special legal situation. It is possible for the Institute for Justice or its ally, The Rutherford Institute (headquartered in Charlottesville, Virginia), to attract such a case because they invite and welcome inquiries on the Internet.[295]

Another possible internal change is for lawyers to accept the fact that the courts will use a rational basis review and then to set out to show that the defendant school district is not even meeting that low standard of performance. The lawyers could, as suggested earlier in regard to the three lawsuits already litigated, examine the educational and legal literature and then try to demonstrate that the challenged school district is not meeting the recommendations made by experienced and expert proponents of community service programs.

The next chapter looks at some possible external changes, concentrating on proposed and recent legislation.

---

[295] The Internet addresses of the Institute for Justice and the Rutherford Institute are, respectively, <http://www.ij.org> and <http://www.rutherford.org>. The Rutherford Institute says on its home page, "Do you need legal assistance? The Rutherford Institute defends civil liberties of all people governed by the United States Constitution. If you are experiencing interference with your rights under the Bill of Rights, please contact us.... The Rutherford Institute stands ready to challenge community service requirements if they should burden religious beliefs or practices." It was the Rutherford Institute that backed and represented Brittney Kaye Settle, a high school freshman, who, after not being permitted to write a term paper on the life of Jesus, sued her school district for violation of her First Amendment rights. *See* Hyman, "Student's Claim to Free Speech v. Teacher's Ordinary Authority," 17 *Illinois School Law Quarterly* 82, 98 (1997).

Chapter V: Proposed and New Legislation

Introduction

This chapter will present several legislative attempts, some successful and some failed, to strengthen parental rights.[296] As mentioned at the end of the previous chapter's commentary on the *Steirer*, *Immediato*, and *Herndon* cases, the court battles over mandatory community service appear to be over unless some internal and external changes occur. In chapter IV, two possible internal changes were presented but neither so far has reached the courtroom. Some of the possible external changes, which are the focus of this chapter, are already evident. They concern parental rights, the basis of one claim of the five brought against mandatory community service, for which there already exists support and an organization devoted to their strengthening. Led by Of the People Foundation, headquartered in Arlington, Virginia,[297] individuals and allied organizations, such as Eagle Forum and Christian Coalition, have supported new federal and state legislative bills. The most publicized bill by a legislature was the federal Parental Rights and Responsibilities Act of 1995 (PRRA) introduced simultaneously in the House of Representatives and the Senate. The most publicized attempt to amend a state constitution by public ballot occurred in Colorado in November 1996. Although both the federal bill and the Colorado amendment proposal failed, these two efforts remain important for the points they raised and the motivation they have given for subsequent legislation.

---

[296] I shall not discuss the National and Community Service Act of 1990 or the National and Community Service Trust Act of 1993. They do not primarily concern community service through a high school program. Nor do they have any apparent legal effect on students opposing mandatory service programs.

[297] The Internet address for Of the People Foundation is <http://www.Ofthepeople.org>.

The Proposed Parental Rights and Responsibilities Act of 1995

On June 28, 1995, Representative Steve Largent of Oklahoma introduced into the House of Representatives a bill, H. R. 1946, "to protect the fundamental right of a parent to direct the upbringing of a child, and for other purposes." On June 29, Senator Charles Grassley of Iowa introduced virtually the same bill into the Senate as S. 984. (Because the differences between the two bills are minor, only Rep. Largent's House of Representatives bill will appear here and be referred to.) The bill, the Parental Rights and Responsibility Act of 1995, was referred subsequently to the Subcommittee on the Constitution of the House Committee on the Judiciary. It appears below in its entirety.

104TH CONGRESS
1ST SESSION

H.R. 1946
To protect the fundamental right of a parent
to direct the upbringing of a child, and for other purposes.

IN THE HOUSE OF REPRESENTATIVES

June 28, 1995

A BILL

To protect the fundamental right of a parent to direct the up-bringing of a child, and for other purposes.
Be it enacted by the Senate and House of Representatives of the United States of America in Congress assembled

SECTION 1. SHORT TITLE.

This Act may be cited as the "Parental Rights and Responsibilities Act of 1995."

SEC.2.FINDINGS AND PURPOSES.

(a)FINDINGS.—Congress finds that—

(1) the Supreme Court has regarded the right of parents to direct the upbringing of their children as a fundamental right implicit in the concept of ordered liberty within the 14th Amendment to the Constitution of the United States, as specified in *Meyer v. Nebraska*, 262 U.S. 390 (1923) and *Pierce v. Society of Sisters*, 268 U.S. 510 (1925);

(2) the role of parents in the raising and rearing of their children is of inestimable value and deserving of both praise and protection by all levels of government;

(3) the tradition of western civilization recognizes that parents have the responsibility to love, nurture, train, and protect their children;

(4) some decisions of Federal and State courts have treated the right of parents not as a fundamental right but as a nonfundamental right, resulting in an improper standard of judicial review being applied to government conduct that adversely affects parental rights and prerogatives;

(5) parents face increasing intrusions into their legitimate decisions and prerogatives by government agencies in situations that do not involve traditional understandings of abuse or neglect but simply are a conflict of parenting philosophies;

(6) governments should not interfere in the decisions and actions of parents without compelling justification; and

(7) the traditional 4-step process used by courts to evaluate cases concerning the right of parents described in paragraph (1) appropriately balances the interests of parents, children, and government.

(b) PURPOSES—The purposes of this Act are—

(1)to protect the right of parents to direct the upbringing of their children as a fundamental right;

(2)to protect children from abuse and neglect as the terms have been traditionally defined and applied in statutory law, such protection being a compelling government interest;

(3) while protecting the rights of parents, to acknowledge that the rights involve responsibilities and specifically

that parents have the responsibility to see that their children are educated, for the purposes of literacy and self-sufficiency, as specified by the Supreme Court in Wisconsin v. Yoder, 406 U.S. 205 (1972);

(4) to preserve the common law tradition that allows parental choices to prevail in a health care decision for a child unless, by neglect or refusal, the parental decision will result in danger to the child's life or result in serious physical injury of the child;

(5) to fix a standard of judicial review for parental rights, leaving to the courts the application of the rights in particular cases based on the facts of the cases and law as applied to the facts; and

(6) to reestablish a 4-step process to evaluate cases concerning the right of parents described in paragraph (1) that—

(A) requires a parent to initially demonstrate that—

(i) the action in question arises from the right of the parent to direct the upbringing of a child; and

(ii) a government has interfered with or usurped the right; and

(B) shifts the burdens of production and persuasion to the government to demonstrate that—

(i) the interference or usurpation is essential to accomplish a compelling governmental interest; and

(ii) the method of intervention or usurpation used by the government is the least restrictive means of accomplishing the compelling interest.

SEC.3.DEFINITIONS.

As used in this Act:

(1) APPROPRIATE EVIDENCE—The term "appropriate evidence" means—

(A) for a case in which a government seeks a temporary or preliminary action or order, except cases which terminate parental custody or visitation, evidence that demonstrates probable cause; and

(B) for a case in which the government seeks a final action or order, or in which it seeks to terminate parental custody or visitation, clear and convincing evidence.

(2) CHILD—The term "child" has the meaning provided by State law.

(3) PARENT—The term "parent" has the meaning provided by State law.

(4) RIGHT OF PARENT TO DIRECT THE UPBRINGING OF A CHILD—

(A) IN GENERAL—The term "right of a parent to direct the upbringing of a child" includes, but is not limited to a right of a parent regarding—

(i) directing or providing for the education of the child;

(ii) making a health care decision for the child, except as provided in subparagraph (B);

(iii) disciplining the child, including reasonable corporal discipline, except as provided in subparagraph (C); and

(iv) directing or providing for the religious teaching of the child.

(B) NO APPLICATION TO PARENTAL DECISIONS ON HEALTH CARE—
The term "right of a parent to direct the upbringing of a child" shall not include a right of a parent to make a decision on health care for the child that, by neglect or refusal, will result in danger to the life of the child or in serious physical injury to the child.

(C) NO APPLICATION TO ABUSE AND NEGLECT—The term "right of a parent to direct the upbringing of a child" shall not include a right of a parent to act or refrain from acting in a manner that constitutes abuse or neglect of a child, as the terms have traditionally been defined.

(5) STATE—The term "State" includes the District of Columbia, the Commonwealth of Puerto Rico, and each territory and possession of the United States.

SEC.4.PROHIBITION ON INTERFERING WITH OR USURPING RIGHTS OF PARENTS.

No Federal, State, or local government, or any official of such a government acting under color of law, shall interfere with or usurp the right of a parent to direct the upbringing of the child of the parent.

SEC.5.STRICT SCRUTINY.

No exception to section 4 shall be permitted, unless the government or official is able to demonstrate, by appropriate evidence, that the interference or usurpation is essential to accomplish a compelling governmental interest and is narrowly drawn or applied in a manner that is the least restrictive means of accomplishing the compelling interest.

SEC.6.CLAIM OR DEFENSE.

Any parent may raise a violation of this Act in an action in a Federal or State court, or before an administrative tribunal, of appropriate jurisdiction as a claim or a defense.

SEC.7.DOMESTIC RELATIONS CASES AND DISPUTES BETWEEN PARENTS.

This Act shall not apply to—
(1)domestic relations cases concerning the appointment of parental rights between parents in custody disputes; or
(2)any other dispute between parents.

SEC.8.ATTORNEY'S FEES.

Subsections(b) and (c) of section 722 of the Revised Statutes (42U.S.C. 1988 (b) and (c)) (concerning the award of attorney's and expert fees) shall apply to cases brought or defended under this Act. A person who uses this Act to defend against a suit by a government described in section 4 shall be construed to be the plaintiff for the purposes of the application of such subsections.

The reader no doubt noted, among other points, the references to three key decisions of the Supreme Court regarding parental rights, *Meyer*, *Pierce*, and *Yoder*; the use of the expression "right of parents to direct the upbringing of their children" (which comes from *Pierce*, as discussed earlier in Chapter 3); the four areas that the parental right includes, pursuant to its definition in Section 3(4)(A); the assertion that the parental right is fundamental according to the Supreme Court; and the specification of the strict scrutiny standard of judicial review to be applied by the courts in litigation involving parental rights. Given the prior discussion of the issues in the lawsuits on mandatory community service, the essential substantive provisions of PRRA are in Sections 4 and 5, after the definitions of terms in Section 3.

Testimony pro and con before the Subcommittee on the Constitution occurred on October 26, 1995. A sampling of four presentations to the Subcommittee follows. Among those supporting PRRA was Greg Erken who identified himself as the Executive Director of Of the People and Rep. Steve Largent as "Of the People's National Vice Chairman."[298] Erken saw the bill as a "much-needed redress to what has become a systematic violation of parental rights." He cited violations in psychological tests given to students in schools and in the distribution of condoms to minors in high schools "without parental notice or consent." He saw the primary role of parents in raising children protected by PRRA, specifically the provision to give "better standing" in court "by making explicit the proper legal standard" to be applied.

Rep. Largent testified as a parent on behalf of PRRA.[299] He stated that PRRA "supports families because it supports parents faced with the challenge of raising children in an increasingly hostile world....The Parental Rights and Responsibilities Act is needed because the government is using its coercive force to dictate values, offend the religious and moral beliefs of families, and restrict the freedom of families to live as they choose." He cited several instances of government coercion against parents, including the treatment of Aric Herndon by his board of education regarding community service.

Rep. Largent pointed out the two critical things PRRA does to protect families: "reaffirmation" of parental rights as "fundamental rights" and specification of the "four-part, bifurcated civil liberties test" in Section 2b(6).[300] These provisions, he said, would provide "no protection for abusing parents." At the same time it "gets the government off the backs of Americans." The provisions of PRRA encouraged American families to act responsibly under protection of the law.

---

[298] Testimony available on the Internet at <http.//www.house.gov/judiciary/2129.htm>
[299] Testimony available on the Internet at <http://www.house.gov/judiciary/2135.htm>
[300] Senator Grassley emphasized this four-part process in his testimony before the subcommittee on the Constitution, available on the Internet at <http://www.house.gov/judiciary/2132.htm> Grassley.

Testimony offered against PRRA countered the advocates' positions by indicating some of the potential and probable negative consequences of the bill. A lengthy and detailed statement opposing PRRA came from Barbara Bennett Woodhouse, Professor of Law at the University of Pennsylvania, who specializes in family law both in her teaching and her service to professional organizations.[301] Woodhouse presented eight reasons, each with commentary and illustrations for opposing PRRA even though she supports "the principle of protecting families from unlawful state intrusions." For Woodhouse the bill was "unnecessary" and "harmful" because:

1. The Bill's language is vague and ambiguous, and the process of clarification will result in harmful confusion at the local level and protracted and fiscally ruinous litigation. (She cited such terms as "temporary or preliminary" action, "final action or order," and "terminate" visitation.)

2. The Bill will raise the costs to local communities of protecting children from abuse and physical or medical neglect.

3. The high costs of losing a PRRA case will deter agencies from making those critical decisions regarding emergency intervention.

4. By using such terms as "traditional" and "physical risk" the PRRA does not succeed in its attempt to distinguish necessary from overly intrusive interventions, and may impede state and local government from responding to new scientific knowledge about child development and children at risk.

5. The PRRA mistakenly focuses narrowly on parents' rights, rather than family rights, and will have tragic unintended consequences for children living with extended families.

---

[301] Woodhouse had written a 127-page law review article, "Who Owns the Child? Meyer and Pierce and the Child as Property," 33 *William and Mary Law Review* 995 (Summer 1992). One key statement in her article concerned the theory behind the Meyer and Pierce decisions that were both written by Justice McReynolds: "As crafted by Justice McReynolds, the thrust of the new constitutional theory of child, parent, and state was deeply conservative, to sustain traditional patriarchal structures and the property interests of schools and teachers, in a society threatened by radical social reform." Id. at 1085. McReynolds' two opinions form the basis of the proposed PRRA in fundamental language.

6. The PRRA neglects any mention of children's rights, either to protection of their family integrity or to protection from harm.
7. The PRRA will have a chilling effect on adoption.
8. Awards of attorney's fees would shift cases involving children away from a focus on cooperating to protect children's interests and towards a focus on the adversarial process.[302]

Also testifying against the PRRA was Vicki Rafel, a member of the Board of Directors of the National Parent Teacher Association. Rafel stated that although the National PTA supported parents rights it saw PRRA "as an unnecessary infringement on the rights of states and localities to take necessary action to protect children, and parents to petition those governments to provide that protection as needed." According to Rafel, the PRRA would jeopardize "the health, welfare, and education of children by removing from them the protection of the law if actions of uninformed parents put them at risk." She questioned the appropriateness of the government defining parental rights when parental rights advocates agreed that the government should not be involved in curtailing parental rights.

The bill never left the Subcommittee on the Constitution.

The Proposed Colorado Parental Rights Amendment

On November 5, 1996, the citizens of Colorado voted on a proposed parental rights amendment to their state constitution. Called for short, Amendment 17, the proposal declared that parents have the natural, essential, and inalienable right to direct and control the upbringing, education, values, and discipline of their children. The proposal, the only state constitutional amendment for parental rights voted on so far, was presented as follows (Language in the proposal was language to be added to the Colorado constitu-

---

[302] Testimony available on the Internet at <http://www.house.gov/judiciary/2139.htm>

tion. Words that appear in all capital letters indicate new material to be added; the word in strike-type indicates material to be deleted):

> Be it Enacted by the People of the State of Colorado:
> Article II, section 3 of the Colorado constitution is amended to read:
> (3)Inalienable rights. All persons have certain natural, essential, and inalienable rights, among which may be reckoned the right of enjoying and defending their lives and liberties; of acquiring, possessing and protecting property; ~~and~~ of seeking and obtaining their safety and happiness; AND OF PARENTS TO DIRECT AND CONTROL THE UPBRINGING, EDUCATION, VALUES, AND DISCIPLINE OF THEIR CHILDREN.

The Legislative Council of the Colorado General Assembly prepared an analysis of the proposed Amendment 17, consisting of brief sections on Background, Arguments For, and Arguments Against.[303] At the beginning of its analysis the Legislative Council included its standard notice that it "takes no position with respect to the merits of the proposals. In listing the 'arguments for' and 'arguments against,' the Council is merely describing the arguments relating to the proposals...."

The Legislative Council presented four arguments for and four arguments against the proposed Parental Rights Amendment. Excerpts follow:

Arguments For:

1. The amendment is intended to affirm the individual, natural, and inalienable rights of parents in raising their children. Constitutional recognition of parental rights can ensure that these rights will not be undermined by the legal, political, educational, and medical systems.

2. Colorado public schools will be more accountable to parents and not be allowed to infringe on parental values and authority.

3. By restoring traditional parental authority, the integ-

---

[303] Analysis available on the Internet on the Colorado home page at <http://www.state.co.us/gov___dir/leg___dir/96bp/amd17.html>

rity and solidarity of the family unit is protected against intrusive outside forces.
4. The proposal will establish legal protection for parents when faced with excessive actions of the government....The amendment...does provide a statement of policy that the rights of parents must be given greater consideration.

Arguments Against:
1. The language of the amendment is broad and raises uncertainty as to how it may be applied....The words *discipline, values, upbringing,* and even *parent* are unclear.
2. This proposal may negatively impact public education.
3. Public health may be endangered. It could limit the rights of minors to access confidential medical services, drug or alcohol addiction treatment, suicide prevention, and possibly emergency medical services.
4. Laws regarding the protection of children may be weakened or set aside.

The voters in Colorado defeated the proposed amendment, with 57 percent against the amendment.

Other Legislation

Two successful pieces of legislation are of note. In Texas in June 1997, Governor George W. Bush signed into law the Child Protective Services Reauthorization Act (Senate Bill 359). The Act was amended on the floor of the Texas House of Representatives, as introduced by State Representative Charlie F. Howard from District 26 (Sugar Land, Texas). The pertinent part of the Act deals with Section 40.052, Duties of the Department of Protective and Regulatory Services Relating to Delivery Services under Chapter 40 of the Human Resources Code. The amended section in pertinent part now reads (underlined words indicate the added language):

Sec. 40.052. The department shall:

(1)propose and implement service delivery standards for departmental programs. *Delivery standards shall not contradict the fundamental right of parents to direct the education and upbringing of their children.*[304]

Thus, the State of Texas now has a statute recognizing that the right of parents established in *Pierce* is fundamental, as set forth in language based on the *Pierce* decision itself. For Rep. Howard it was important to indicate that the parental right is a fundamental one. Alluding to the distinction between fundamental and non-fundamental rights, Howard grouped First Amendment free speech and free exercise of religion with the parental right to rear children: "Fundamental rights include things like free speech and the free exercise of religion, concepts which help form the definition of who we are as a culture. It is only right that these rights be protected and that we place a high burden of proof on the state in order to override these rights."[305]

Rep. Howard defended his amendment by declaring:

Protecting the integrity of the family should be among the highest priorities of any government....It is right that a high wall of separation be maintained between the state and the family. If a parent's right to direct the upbringing of their children is not fundamental, the door is wide open for the state to interfere in families and control any number of non-critical decisions. If our system failed to recognize parents' rights as fundamental, children would no longer be distinguishable from coal or oil or lumber; they become simply one more resource to be managed.[306]

In January 1996, Governor John Engler of Michigan signed into law new language for the Michigan Public School Code. The added section, sponsored by the State Representative Harold Voorhees of the 77th District (Wyoming, Michigan), is as follows:

---

[304] *Protecting Parents' Rights: Defending the Howard Amendment* 1, announcement by State of Texas Representative Charlie F. Howard.

[305] *Id.* at 2.

[306] *Id.*

Section 380.10 Rights of parents and legal guardians; duties of public schools.
It is the natural, fundamental right of parents and legal guardians to determine and direct the care, teaching, and education of their children. The public schools of this state serve the needs of the pupils by cooperating with the pupil's parents and legal guardians to develop the pupil's intellectual capabilities and vocational skills in a safe and positive environment. (Effective July 1, 1996.)[307]

With this new section, Michigan has language in its Education Code specifying that the parental right is natural and fundamental. The language, while based on the language in *Pierce*, is somewhat more expansive than the *Pierce* declaration of the parental right. It gives parents the right to "determine and direct" the education of their children while specifying that the public schools "cooperate" with the parents to develop a pupil's capabilities and vocational skills. While Rep. Voorhees hoped to use more extensive language, he finally settled for the language above in the code in order to make his proposal acceptable to a majority of the Michigan House of Representatives.[308]

Commentary on the Legislation

The people, the zeitgeist, and the organizations that supported the plaintiffs in *Steirer, Immediato,* and *Herndon* against mandatory community service are virtually the same as those people and groups who support the new and proposed legislation to strengthen parental rights. The specific names of individuals in the headlines are different, but the language used and the organizations are the same. The rationale for the Fourteenth Amendment parental rights claim in the lawsuits is the same as the rationale for amending a state constitution or passing a new statute in Congress or in a state legislature. Naturally, the reactions of the defenders of mandatory community service are essentially the same as those of the opponents to legislation on parental rights,

---

[307] Michigan Revised School Code, §380.10.
[308] Letter dated May 11, 1998, from one of Representative Voorhees's legislative aides.

except that opponents to the new legislation raise family and child protection issues in addition to education issues.

Consider two reactions against the Parental Rights and Responsibilities Act. August Steinhilber, former general counsel for the National School Boards Association headquartered in Washington, D.C., called the proposed PRRA "another lawyers' relief act or full employment act." Steinhilber went on to say,

> And it would raise total havoc with the curriculum. The irony is that everyone is saying the curriculum should be enriched and broadened, but this would give parents veto power over almost anything they didn't like....If you start looking for everything that's objectionable to someone's values, you could throw out the whole curriculum.[309]

The National Education Association, also headquartered in Washington, D.C., issued a statement and lengthy critique of the components of the proposed PRRA, with citations of lawsuits relevant to each point. That statement's opening, general paragraph was:

> The Parental Rights and Responsibilities Act (S. 984 and H.R. 1496) represents an unprecedented effort to impose *federal* control over *local* school affairs. This legislation is disruptive, intrusive, expensive, and unnecessary, and will wreak havoc in the public schools. We urge its defeat.[310] [emphasis in the original.]

Compare the above language of the two reactions by Steinhilber and the National Education Association against the PRRA with the language of Judge Brieant in rejecting the *Immediato* plaintiffs' Fourteenth Amendment claim against mandatory community service. Judge Brieant said:

> No public policy will be served by this Court usurping the legitimate authority of school officials to perform their duties in educating citizens; to attempt to do so, because we, or Plaintiffs, consider the Program undesirable on purely secular grounds would *wreak havoc* in the administration of the schools, and involve the federal judiciary impermissibly in matters of local Home Rule.[311] [emphasis added].

---

[309] *The New York Times,* May 1, 1996, at A1 and B7.
[310] Statement of the National Education Association Regarding the Parental Rights and Responsibilities Act, February 1996.
[311] Immediato I, 873 F. Supp. at 852.

The parents and politicians who are supporting new legislation are using the political arena to achieve what they have failed to do through persuasion and court decisions. In essence, they are responding to the invitation (or challenge, depending on one's interpretation) sent by the judges who ruled against them. Judge Brieant in accepting the *Steirer* court's decision when he, too, rejected the students'involuntary servitude claim, said, "...we rely on the continued existence of the right to petition local officials for an exemption or limitation of the Program and the retained right, if Plaintiffs and a majority of their neighbors find the Program too oppressive, to 'throw the rascals out' at the next school board election."[312] Judge Bullock, in rejecting the *Herndon* plaintiffs' claims, likewise said, "Plaintiffs retain the right to seek change by supporting, along with their neighbors, school board candidates who would cancel or revise the community service program."[313]

The advocates of the new legislation seek to use enacted law as protection from what they see as intrusion by governmental agencies into the realm of families. They agree that everyone needs a government to organize, protect, and provide citizens with social benefits. At the same time they are keen to secure and even enlarge that part of family life into which the government may not and should not enter. They cite and agree with the Supreme Court's statement in *Prince,*

> It is cardinal with us that the custody, care, and nurture of the child reside first in the parents, whose primary function and freedom include preparation for obligations the state can neither supply nor hinder....And it is in recognition of this that these decisions [referring to *Barnette, Meyer,* and *Pierce*] have respected the private realm of family life which the state cannot enter.[314]

The advocates recognize, as they must, the eternal tension between individual/family rights and legitimate governmental rights, but they prefer more independence from governmental requirements and actions for the welfare of the larger society. It is a matter of preference and perception. Sen. Grassley, who introduced PRRA in the Senate put it this way: "This bill is not an education bill. It's an individual liberties versus government bill."[315]

---

[312] *Id.* at 851.
[313] Herndon I, 899 F. Supp. at 1455.
[314] Prince v. Massachusetts, 321 U.S. 158, 166, 64 S. Ct. 438, 442, 88 L. Ed. 645, 652-653 (1944).
[315] *The New York Times*, May 1, 1996, at A1 and B7.

The concrete purpose of the Act comes out in a statement by one of the leaders of a group influential in supporting, if not initiating, the drive for the new legislation. "What we're trying to insure through this legislation is very simple: that schools reinforce rather than undermine the values parents teach to our children in our homes, churches, and synagogues," said Ralph Reed, head of the Christian Coalition which supported the PRRA bill.[316]

The drafters of the PRRA, as well as the drafters of the later proposed Colorado Parental Rights Amendment, the Texas Child Protective Services statute, and the Michigan Education Code, tactically built upon favorable Supreme Court language. They did not succeed, however, in presenting clear and specific language that would yield an acceptable balance among parental, child, and governmental interests. Even some supporters of parental rights, like Woodhouse and Rafel who testified against PRRA, saw that the proposed legislation would bring, unintentionally and ironically, further governmental intrusion through litigation in court over the meaning of the Act's key terms, including the terms *direct the upbringing* and *traditional*. That is to say, it would require further governmental effort to define the terms of an act designed to lessen governmental interference in family life.

The PRRA, despite its title, did not specify how parents would be held accountable for what the bill itself states are the responsibilities of the parents according to the tradition of western civilization—"to love, nurture, train, and protect their children."[317] That is, Sections 4, 5, 6, and 7 of the PRRA deal with parental rights, following the three sections dealing with title, findings and purposes, and definitions. The PRRA had no provision specifying what federal action would occur or be possible. Nor did the PRRA deal with the rights of children or extended families, as pointed out in testimony and as voiced elsewhere. As Shirley Igo, the Vice President for Legislation of the National PTA said, "There's a very fine balance between the rights of parents and the rights of children. We're strong advocates for parents' responsibility and involvement, but this tips the balance where only parents' rights are protected."[318]

---

[316] *Id.*

[317] PRRA, §2(a)(3).

[318] *The New York Times*, May 1, 1996, at A1 and B7.

In addition, had the PRRA passed, there would have been a jurisprudential issue with PRRA. The PRRA declared, citing *Meyer* and *Pierce*, that the parental right to direct the upbringing of children is a "fundamental right"[319] and that in litigation the courts must apply a "compelling governmental interest"[320] test when reviewing the action being challenged. However, although the Act declared parental rights to be fundamental, the Supreme Court in *Meyer* and *Pierce* did not state that the parental right was fundamental and did not require a strict scrutiny test. Rather, the Court after making the oft-repeated and now classic statement in *Pierce* about the liberty of parents "to direct the upbringing and education of children" indicated that the appropriate standard of review is the rational basis. The Court stated that the parental right "may not be abridged by legislation which has no *reasonable relation* to some purpose within the competency of the state."[321] [emphasis added].

Based on this situation, when faced with the request in *Brown* to declare parental rights to be fundamental, the First Circuit Court of Appeals reviewed the *Meyer* and *Pierce* decisions and concluded that "the Supreme Court has yet to decide whether the right to direct the upbringing and education is among those fundamental rights whose infringement merit heightened scrutiny."[322] The *Brown* court indicated its own opinion by refusing to declare the parental right to be fundamental.[323] (Similarly, Immediato and Herndon urged their courts to declare the parent's right to be fundamental in order to justify a strict scrutiny test which they believed would help their cause.)

Thus, the question arises whether Congress would have had the power to declare successfully via this PRRA legislation that the parental right is a fundamental right and to specify to the courts the highest level of review in their adjudications. A similar question about the power of Congress arose recently in *City of Boerne v. Flores*, a case dealing with the Religious Freedom Restoration Act of 1993 (RFRA). There the Supreme Court ruled, in part, that Congress exceeded its authority and upset the traditional separation of powers between Congress and the Judiciary by requiring a compelling interest test.[324]

---

[319] PRRA, §2(a)(1).
[320] PRRA §2(b)(6)(B) and §5.
[321] Pierce, 268 U.S. at 535-536.
[322] Brown, 68 F. 3d at 533.
[323] *Id.*
[324] 521 U.S. 507, 117 S.Ct. 2157, 138 L.Ed. 2d 624 (1997).

In this way, the PRRA as proposed might well have led to further litigation, not less, about parental rights. If PRRA had been enacted, would Congress have exceeded its authority by interpreting the constitution about what is a fundamental right and what standard of review to apply, a role of the Judiciary not the Congress?

For all of the reasons above, including: (1)lack of support from an essential constituent group, the National PTA; (2)opposition from health care advocates, women's groups, child and youth advocates, and educators (among them the National Education Association and American Association of School Administrators); and (3)the question of constitutionality of central elements of the PRRA, the proposed legislation failed to leave the House's Judiciary Committee. As a result, PRRA is dead in Congress at this point.

A related bill (H.R. 3189) now exists, The Parental Freedom of Information Act (PFIA), sponsored by Representative Todd Tiahrt of Kansas. (Rep. Steve Largent is a co-sponsor of Tiahrt's bill as was Tiahrt of Largent's PRRA.) The new bill, introduced in the House of Representatives on February 11, 1998, proposes to amend the Family Education Rights and Privacy Act of 1974 "to further define the right of parents to guide the education of their children. This legislation is vital to providing parents of public school children with a clear-cut right to access of information regarding the content of the education their children are receiving."[325] This legislation has been endorsed by the Heritage Foundation, Family Research Council, Of the People Foundation, and Focus on the Family.[326]

Recognizing the defeat of the attempt to pass the Parental Rights and Responsibilities Act and its limitations, even if it were passed, the proponents of parental rights have shifted their energy and attention to the passage of amendments to state constitutions. This policy shift occurs in spite of any successes in passing state statutes or state regulations, like the two successful ones in Texas and Michigan mentioned earlier that declare parental rights to be a fundamental right. The proponents realize that

---

[325] Legislative Analysis sheet distributed by Representative Todd Tiahrt of Kansas.
[326] Material distributed by Representative Tiahrt's office, Feb. 11, 1998.

anything less than a state constitutional amendment suffers from possible limitations of scope. That is, state statutes, like the Texas one, most often are not broadly based but narrowly confined to a child protection act or education act context.[327] Such a condition limits the rights of parents. Moreover, such statutes are subject to the judges' interpretation of constitutionality concerning what is a fundamental right and what is the appropriate standard of judicial review.

By definition, a state constitutional amendment would have a broad scope of applicability and would not be subject to litigation in court as to constitutionality. Given that a change in federal law—federal constitution or federal statute—does not seem possible at this point, changes in state constitutions even with their scopes limited to one state each, do deserve attention because they appear to be possible. As of this writing, the latest state in which a Parental Rights Amendment has been introduced is Connecticut (February, 1998), making it the 29th state.[328]

The advocates of parental rights have learned from their defeat in Colorado and have taken steps to correct their errors. The critical error was the phrasing of the proposed amendment. The Of the People Foundation in 1994 introduced model language for a state Parental Rights Amendment based on the *Pierce* decision. The model language reads:

1. The right of parents to direct the upbringing and education of their children shall not be infringed.
2. The legislature shall have power to enforce, by appropriate legislation, the provision of this article.[329]

Nevertheless, the Colorado proponents of a state parental rights constitutional amendment introduced a ballot initiative with different language to amend their constitution's section on inalien-

---

[327] Interview with Robert C. Heckman, Senior Vice-President of Of the People Foundation, in Arlington, Virginia, on April 17, 1998. *See also* Robert C. Heckman and Shannon Royce, Parental Rights: Establishing the Legal Groundwork for School Choice 2 (Sept. 9, 1997).

[328] Announcement released by Of the People Foundation, February 25, 1998. Almost all of the introduced proposed amendments have died and not been reintroduced into new legislative sessions.

[329] Of the People Foundation, The Parental Rights Amendment: Evolution of Model Language. (undated). [written after January 1997.]

able rights. The ballot initiative, repeated here from the earlier section for ease of comparison, was as follows:

"All persons have certain natural, essential and inalienable rights, among which may be reckoned the right of enjoying and defending their lives and liberties; of acquiring, possessing and protecting property; and of seeking and obtaining their safety and happiness; AND OF PARENTS TO DIRECT AND CONTROL THE UPBRINGING, EDUCATION, VALUES, AND DISCIPLINE OF THEIR CHILDREN."

Several deviations from the 1994 model language of Of the People are significant. First, the proposed Colorado amendment language referred to the parental right as a natural, essential, and inalienable right, not a fundamental right. When a right is a fundamental one, the government can limit that right with legislation that demonstrates a compelling interest in the matter being challenged and by narrowly tailoring the limitation to achieve that compelling interest. In contrast, inalienable rights are absolute rights, ones which are "not capable of being surrendered or transferred without the consent of the one possessing such rights."[330]

Second, the proposed Colorado amendment included the terms values and discipline, giving parents an inalienable right to direct and control their children's values and discipline. This language would have allowed parents an easy way to try to avoid child abuse claims against them. A parent might say, "I was just disciplining my child, not abusing him." Prosecution for child abuse would have become difficult. Third, the proposed amendment went beyond the Supreme Court language in *Pierce* by shifting the term control to a different position. The *Pierce* court said that parents have the "right to direct the upbringing and education of children under their control."

In sum, the proposed amendment declared that parents have a right "to direct and control the upbringing, education, values, and discipline of their children." This shift in language away from the 1994 model language had its negative effect, as shown by a newspaper report of a statement by a spokeswoman for the Colorado Association of School Boards. According to the report, the spokeswoman "also maintained that the language of the measure—by ensuring parents' 'control' of their children's education—would ultimately have moved education in the state toward a voucher system."[331]

---

[330] *Black's Law Dictionary* 683 (5th ed. 1979).
[331] *Education Week*, Nov. 13, 1996, at 1.

In January 1997, just two months after the defeat of the proposed amendment to the Colorado constitution in November 1996,
the Of the People Foundation formulated and adopted new model
language reflecting the criticism of the proposed Colorado amendment. The new model language is:

1. The right of the parents to direct the upbringing and
   education of their children is a fundamental right.
2. The state maintains a compelling interest in investigating, prosecuting, and punishing child abuse and
   neglect as defined by statute.[332]

With this 1997 language, advocates of a state constitutional
amendment believe that they will not be subject in the future to
strong opposition regarding child abuse and will be able to lead
their fellow citizens to approve an initiative on parental rights.
This new model language is the language used in the proposed
state constitutional amendment introduced in Connecticut in February, 1998.

In addition to the errors regarding language of the proposed
amendment, the amendment advocates failed to enlist sufficient
support from Colorado voters. The pro-amendment campaign
was funded and supported in large measure by out-of-state people.
The Coalition for Parental Responsibility, established in April 1996
to lead the campaign supporting the amendment, raised as of the
end of October 1996, $463,000. Of that sum 99 percent came from
out-of-state, 80 percent of it from Of the People. (The Coalition
received $77,500 from Of the People to hire professional petition
circulators in April.)[333] This contrasts starkly to the funds raised
by the Protect Our Children Coalition which opposed the amendment. The Coalition received 88 percent of its money, $334,000
(also as of the end of October 1996) from in-state donors.[334]

Not only was general voter support lacking from within the
state. The governor of Colorado, Roy Romer, and other prominent state officials opposed the amendment. Local librarians, video
store owners, and bookstore owners opposed the amendment because they feared lawsuits from parents. One bookstore owner

---

[332] Of the People Foundation, *supra* note 334.
[333] *The New York Times*, November 4, 1996, at A14.
[334] *Id.*

said, "How are bookstores, record stores, or video stores supposed to know if a book, or record, or movie violates a parents' right to 'direct and control' the education and values of their children?"[335] Gov. Romer, using language reminiscent of Steinhilber's reaction to PRRA about nine months earlier, said, "It's explosive in its ambiguity. The only thing certain about it is that it's going to lead to very expensive lawsuits. This is a full employment bill for lawyers."[336]

The reaction from Jeffrey Bell, Chairman of Of the People was an admission that the campaign for the amendment was mishandled. He said, "I've learned a lot of lessons in this defeat. We needed more support from state officers—the governor and senators."[337] Bell also expressed this lessons-were-learned theme in his column "From the Chairman," published in the newsletter of Of the People Foundation.[338] The defeat was a bitter one for Bell, who earlier had said, "Victory here 'could be more important than Dole's election or the control of Congress.'"[339](Senator Robert Dole, the Republican candidate for president in 1996, had endorsed the amendment when campaigning in Colorado,[340]as he had the PRRA earlier.[341] Dole won against President Clinton in Colorado.[342])

In summary, the attempts to pass a federal statute, the Parental Rights and Responsibilities Act of 1995, and a state constitutional amendment in Colorado in November, 1996, failed for a number of reasons, including lack of support, ambiguous language, and vocal opposition. The proponents of parental rights, however, are continuing their efforts to succeed in passing statutes and amendments that will reflect and influence continued opposition to perceived governmental intrusion into family life in America. At this point it is not clear where and if proponents will succeed in their mission.

Nor is it clear that even with a federal statute, or a state statute, or a state constitutional amendment plaintiff parents will be

---

[335] *Id.*
[336] *Id.*
[337] *Education Week*, November 13, 1996, at 1.
[338] *Voice*, Winter 1997, at 2.
[339] *The New York Times*, November 4, 1996, at A14.
[340] *Education Week*, November 13, 1996, at 1.
[341] *The New York Times*, May 1, 1996, at A1 and B7.
[342] Dole received 691,848 votes (45.8 percent); Clinton received 671,152 votes (44.4 percent); and others received 147,704 votes (9.8 percent). R. Scammon, A. McGillivary, and R. Cook, America Votes 22 (1996): A Handbook of Contemporary American Election Statistics 140 (1998).

able to exempt their children from mandatory community service in high school. The courts might well follow the course taken in the First and Tenth Circuits and circumscribe the rights of parents. That is, the courts might permit parents to direct their children to a particular school or school district but not permit them to control their children's curriculum by picking and choosing which courses to take from among the mandated offerings. Even with new legislation parents will still have to demonstrate that their rights outweigh the interest of the state in operating an administratively reasonable school system for the community as a whole.

Perhaps parental rights advocates will be able to mount other federal and state initiatives to attract nationwide attention. Or, perhaps some other external event will take place to alter the current status of parental rights, thereby altering the future status of lawsuits against mandatory community service as a requirement for graduation from high school. In any case, as contended in the preceding chapter, unless some new internal and external events occur, the legal challenge to mandatory community service has ended.

Chapter VI: Community Service Outcomes: Court Comments, Survey Data, and Student Self-Reflections

Proponents of mandatory community service programs have readily stated their purposes, which are in effect a way of stating their intended outcomes. However, they have not been so ready or forthcoming to provide evidence that their programs have achieved these purposes. When they have offered evidence on outcomes they most often have done so with evidence from other programs gathered by outside researchers. Educators, board of education members, judges, parents, and lawyers still need to look for and request information about the outcomes of initiating community service programs in high school just as they must (or should) look at the consequences of introducing other required programs, such as the study of American history.[343] A moment of reflection will reveal that the measurement and assessment of curricular outcomes is a complex matter. This chapter will take a look at some of the reported outcomes of community service performed by high school students.

Measurement and Evaluation of Outcomes

Without engaging in a lengthy treatment of the questions concerning measurement (for example, What were the outcomes of Program X in 1993?) and the questions concerning policy making (for example, Given the results of Program X, should we, as board of education members, continue to mandate 70 hours of

---

[343] In New Jersey, for example, the state legislature has enacted and amended the following legislation: "The superintendent of schools in each school district shall prepare and recommend to the board of education of the district, and the board of education shall adopt a suitable 2-year course of study in the history of the United States, including the history of New Jersey, to be given to each student during the last 4 years of high school. Said course of study shall include materials recommended by the commissioner dealing with history of the negro in America." (N.J. Stat. 18A:35-1). Subsequent legislation (N.J.Stat. 18A:35-2 and 35-2.1) outlines the "nature and purpose" of that course. I know of no study in the last ten years that measured the outcomes of that required course, evaluated the quality of the courses being offered, and discussed the worthiness of this policy decision.

community service for our high school students?) it is fair to say that the tasks of identifying, measuring, evaluating, and judging the worth of mandatory community service programs are daunting. This statement about community service is true, too, when performing the same tasks for other required courses, such as world civilizations, physical education, mathematics, and foreign language.

The issue of measurement of community service outcomes concerns not only questions about which data to gather such as, which facts, principles, and values did students learn? How did the students feel about performing this service? What did it cost the school to carry out the program? What social, economic, and other civic benefits did the school and the community gain? What programs and activities were not funded, fully or in some measure, as a result of funding the community service program? How did student experiences in community service connect with other aspects of the school's curriculum? To what extent did community service experiences influence decisions about career choices by the students? The issue of measurement also concerns which type of data to gather. That is, will the data come from formal survey instruments completed by the students, or from personal and group interviews of the students, or from written essays or unstructured journal jottings, or from anecdotal reports by teachers, parents, and community people who have had close relations with the participating students? In short, the issue of measurement, as well as the issues of evaluation and policy determination, concern the what and how of data that will be useful in understanding the qualitative and quantitative effects of a community service program and in deciding on the worth of such a program to the students' high school curriculum.

The measurement of outcomes is not easy, and generally individual programs do not gather them systematically. The reason for this state of affairs may well be that the data needed or desired by school leaders are deemed too costly to obtain. It may well be that what is possible to obtain is only a fraction of what is preferred. It also may be that what is needed or desired is not measurable in any precise way much as it is not possible to measure the nature, amount, and effects of love that is claimed to bind family members together. It may be that the people who could gather the data do not have the skills and motivation to gather what other people would be satisfied with. Such is the complexity of measuring an ongoing multifaceted social activity. In any case, local data are conspicuously absent or scarce in the briefs of the parties to the three lawsuits and in the court opinions whereas the purposes of the community service programs are present, overt, and stated adequately.

Community service presents a measurement and evaluation problem because it is not a single task such as memorizing a string of prime members or spelling a list of two-syllable words. With community service it is difficult to define the independent variable to be studied. Because community service affects so many dimensions of a student's life in and out of school, it presents serious challenges to professional researchers who choose to study it. However, the challenges and the lack of local research data on outcomes are not overburdening problems because citizens, board of education members, and educators do not rely 100 percent on research data when making policy decisions about community service and most other school curriculum matters. This situation makes the problems of research bearable. Conrad and Hedin, two prominent researchers on community service, have acknowledged:

> Very little, if anything, has been "proven" by educational research. Advocates of most any practice, be it cooperative learning, team teaching, computer-assisted instruction, or the lecture method, can find research evidence in its favor. Detractors, and empirical purists, can find reasons for discounting the results of most any study. It is doubtful that support from research is the prime cause for the adoption of any educational method—even those most commonly practiced. Educational research is a difficult and complex business and particularly so when service is the target of investigation.[344]

Court Comments, Survey Data, and Student Self-Reflections

In spite of the complexity and difficulty about learning the effects of community service activities, some data are available that give insight for understanding the outcomes of community

---

[344] D. Conrad and D. Hedin, *High School Community Service: A Review of Research and Programs* 20, (Dec. 1989) National Center on Effective Secondary Schools, Madison, WI. ERIC #ED-313-569.

service and their relation to the stated purposes. What follows below is not intended to be a comprehensive review of the literature. It is only a personal sampling, a look at some data and some statements tied closely to the legal dimension of community service programs that is the focus of this particular book. Nevertheless, this sampling does reflect the general literature on community service.

To protect the privacy of people, I shall not identify individual names of the people who are quoted. I will say that all items are taken from court opinions, briefs, affidavits submitted to the courts, publicly available material, or research projects.

Comments from the Court Opinions

1. "[Student's] parents, co-plaintiffs, concede that community service is rewarding, but maintain that it must remain a matter of individual choice."[345]
2. "...it is educational, particularly when coupled with related classroom discussions."[346]
3. "Defendants state that participants in school community service programs have reported 'a positive effect on their concern for fellow human beings, self-motivation to learn, participate, and achieve, sense of usefulness in relation to the community, sense of responsibility to their group, responsibility for their own life, awareness of community problems, communication skills, and sense of confidence, competence, and self-awareness.'"[347]

Survey and Other Quantitative Data

The data on the psychological and social development of student (the first of four purposes of community service identified in Chapter 2) offer the strongest research support for community service. These data overlap the third purpose, civic education, in that the concept of social responsibility that is highlighted in the quantitative research applies to both personal development and civic education.

---

[345] Immediato II, 73 F. 3d at 458.
[346] *Id.* at 460.
[347] Herndon I, , 899 F. Supp. at 1452-3.

In an interim report of the National Evaluation of Learn and Serve America: School and Community-Based Programs data from the 1995-96 school year survey of approximately 1000 middle and high school students indicate "positive, statistically significant impacts on all measures of civic attitudes used in the study, including measures of personal and social responsibility, acceptance of cultural diversity, and service leadership (defined as the degree to which students feel they are aware of needs in a community, are able to develop and implement a service project, and are committed to service now and later in life.)"[348] There was also a marginal significant reduction in teenage pregnancy. "The finding on teenage pregnancy, when coupled with results from other studies, suggests that while service alone may not dramatically reduce risk behaviors, service may contribute to the effectiveness of more comprehensive programs targeted to reducing those behaviors among school-aged youth."[349]

In another study the research indicates that students participating in community service gained in "social responsibility and their sense of personal competence in a modest way."[350] Additionally, participating students gained in "favorable attitudes toward adults and also toward the types of organizations and people with whom they were involved."[351] For junior high students with behavioral difficulties community service yielded "lower levels of alienation and isolation and fewer disciplinary problems."[352]

Research data on intellectual (academic) development, the second purpose of community service identified earlier in Chapter 2, are not as favorable as the psychological and social development data. Nevertheless, the data do support gains by participating students, especially students who tutor students of different ages. (It is common for high schools to permit participating students to tutor younger students during school hours for at least one-half of the program's required number of hours.) In addition, students who participated in political and social action activities became more open-minded.[353] While the data are not as

---

[348] A. Melchior, National Evaluation of Learn and Serve America: School and Community Based Programs, vi-29 (April, 1997).

[349] *Id.*

[350] Newmann and Rutter, *supra* note 20, at 34.

[351] D. Conrad and D. Hedin, "School-based Community Service: What Do We Know from Research and Theory?", 72 Phi Delta Kappan 743,747 (June 1991).

[352] *Id*, reporting on the research by R. Calabrese and H. Schumer, "The Effects of Service Activities on Adolescent Alienation," 21 Adolescence 675 (1986).

[353] Conrad and Hedin, *supra* note 351, at 747.

extensive or supportive for intellectual development as they are for psychological and social development, it is noteworthy that time spent in community service does not detract from classroom learning. "Engaging students in active learning outside the traditional classroom had no negative effects on academic achievement."[354]

In an effort to gather data tied to the three court cases described in Chapter 3, this author surveyed students in a New Jersey public high school. The survey questionnaire (subsequently refined; see below) had two parts. Part 1 consisted of a 30-item list of statements to which students responded on a 4-point scale of Strongly Agree (4), Somewhat Agree (3), Somewhat Disagree (2), and Strongly Disagree (1). Part 2 consisted of one open-ended item seeking information on needed improvement in the student's community service program. The 30-items reflected the author's reading of the literature,[355] interviews with students and teachers, and his view of the learning theory, justifications, and legal issues involved in community service. For example, because of liability and risk management issues, an item about safety training was included; and because Judge Brieant's[356] negative remark about community service in *Immediato I*, an item about the possibility of learning more from an extra course of study than from participation in a community service project was included.

The data came from 87 students in a New Jersey public high school. These students constituted all the students willing and available to complete the survey at a student assembly during the Spring 1997 semester. The students made up about 50 percent of the entire number of students participating in the community service program on that spring day. Computation of mean scores and some crosstabulations, did provide some important information.[357]

---

[354] R.C. Wade, *Community Service-Learning* 31 (1997). Wade cites three research studies, two from the 1970s and one from 1994, to draw this conclusion in his overview of the research about the effectiveness of community service.

[355] Two new, fairly comprehensive edited volumes have appeared in print recently. Rather than cite a long list of separate articles and books, I shall only refer the interested reader to the individual chapters of these books and their various sets of references: Rahima C. Wade, ed., *Community Service-Learning: A Guide to Including Service in the Public School Curriculum* (1997); and Joan Schine, *Service Learning: Ninety-sixth Yearbook of the National Society for the Study of Education, Part 1* (1997).

[356] Immediato, *supra* note 4, 873 F. Supp. at 850.

[357] I thank Professor Douglas Penfield and Gail Verona, doctoral student, for their help in refining the survey instrument and processing the data.

The items with the four highest mean scores (that is, closest to Strongly Agree) were: My family supports my community service (3.58); the community service that I do is meaningful to me (3:45); I believe in the goals of our community service program (3:43); and I feel glad when I do community service through my school (3.38). The items with the four lowest mean scores (that is, closest to Strongly Disagree) were: In my school the community service program is integrated primarily with one of my courses (1.68); I received safety training for my community service work (2.00); I discuss my community service with my teachers, and the discussions help me to understand my service experience better (2.01); and I would be learning more with an extra course instead of performing community service (2.06).

Two crosstabulations of items are of particular note. Items 15 and 7 (integration with a course; personal meaningfulness, respectively) were cross tabulated. In 2x2 crosstabulation matrix (Agree and Disagree for one item crosstabulated with Agree and Disagree of the other item) 75 percent of the students who responded to both questions reported that they found very high personal meaningfulness even though there was very low integration of their service with their courses.

In another, similar crosstabulation of items 14 and 7 (schools should require community service; personal meaningfulness, respectively) 73 percent of the students who answered both questions combined very high personal meaningfulness with agreement that community service should be required. In other words, for these students the requirement of community service did not detract from the high degree of meaningfulness of their service learning project.

The original questionnaire was later refined so that it would tie more closely with the language in the court opinions for the three lawsuits as well as with the four purposes of community service: psychological and social development; intellectual (academic) development; civic education; and goodwill and reform. This version of the survey instrument also has two parts. Part I consists of a list of 25 statements, 6 for each of the four purposes plus one (Item #4) designed to solicit information regarding special training and/or safety training. (Such training we believe relates to the issue of liability, which will be discussed briefly in the next chapter.) (See Figure 9, page 121 -123.)

With the refined version there are data from 71 students who are participating in another New Jersey public high school's community service program. The data are similar to those from the original version. The highest mean score, 3.49, is for item 6 (I believe that community service is admirable and worthwhile), and the lowest mean score, 2.00, is for item 9 (I discuss my service activity with my teachers in one or more of my classes). Again 2x2 crosstabulations obtained results similar to previous results.

The crosstabulation of items 25 and 6 (The service program I participate in has positive effects for our community; I believe that community service is admirable and worthwhile, respectively) is of special interest because of the connection between the civic education purpose (item 25) and the psychological and social development purpose (item 6). Here, 86 percent of the students reported agreement on both of these two items. In other words, almost 7 out of 8 students combined perceived positive value of service with effects, two fundamental concepts in community service programs. The precise relationship between the belief that service is admirable and worthwhile and positive effects of the service activity deserves much further consideration. (See Figure 10, page 124.)

Selected Student Self-Reflections

Students performing community service typically record their experiences in some way. Some note their "special feeling or memories."[358]

Others focus on what they "gained"[359] from their service or what were their first and resulting impressions of the people whom they served.[360] Others keep journals.[361] These self-reflections by students do not offer data from a carefully executed research study. Rather, they offer personal, qualitative descriptions of the impact and outcomes of community service. Such self-reflections present a consistent finding: community service offers a powerful approach to learning, and students learn a great deal from their service activities.[362]

---

[358] See Figure 6, from Chapel Hill High School, page 60.
[359] See Figure 4, from Rye Neck High School, page 58.
[360] See Figure 7, from Chapel Hill High School, page 61.
[361] See Figure 2, from Bethlehem Area School District, page 56.
[362] My own experience, interviews, and research on this point is corroborated by D. Conrad and D. Hedin, *School-Based Community Service: What We Know from Research and Theory*, 72 Phi Delta Kappan 743, 748 (June 1991).

The following sample of excerpts is characteristic of what appears in various research and general reports. The items below purposely come from sources basically inaccessible to virtually all readers: the briefs submitted to the courts during the three lawsuits and an article in a local newspaper that serves the area where one of the lawsuits was filed. Some excerpts are from students participating in the challenged programs, while others are from similar service programs in other schools. These items, appearing in public print here for the first time, complement what is already available to all readers in the general literature.[363]

It is from student statements like the ones that follow that researchers, teachers, parents, and adults draw their generalizations about the qualitative outcomes of community service. As Conrad and Hedin concluded in their review of the available research, including their own, "Evidence from qualitative, anecdotal studies suggests even more strongly and consistently [than evidence from "quantitative methodologies"] that community service can be a worthwhile, useful, enjoyable, and powerful learning experience."[364]

1. "In the past year I have completed over 100 hours of community service, more than fulfilling the H.S. service learning and reflection requirement. I serve for one and one-half hours each week at the Memorial Hospital....I was not previously involved in community service. I began participating in service in order to fulfill the school service learning requirement....I have learned responsibility....Another thing I have learned through service is to be more comfortable and confident working with other people, including people I don't know....I've learned that sick people need and deserve to be treated with equal dignity....

Doing community service has taught me to see myself as someone who can help make things better. I now look at problems in the community and try to think of something that I would like to do about it. I'm definitely going to do more community service in the future. This is part of my life now."

2. "I have performed many hours of community service through my membership in the Girl Scouts and through school

[363] *See* in particular the excerpts in D. Conrad and D. Hedin, *supra* note 344. These excerpts are repeated in a readily available article by the same researchers, *School-Based Community Service: What We Know from the Research and Theory,* 72 Phi Delta Kappan 743, 748 (June 1991).

[364] *Id.* at 746.

organizations....I have come to realize how much a person can learn from real-life, hands-on experience and how important it is to expose students to these experiences...

"[For 13 months] I worked on a project at the local homeless shelter to earn my Girl Scout Silver Award. I installed a small outdoor play area for the children at the shelter....In the course of this project I received and disbursed over $4000, chose appropriate play equipment, and studied local regulations and applied for a town permit. I set and stuck to my own deadlines. I attended meetings and spoke to local organizations in order to gain funds and publicize my project....The lessons and skill I learned are invaluable....I have changed my mind totally on the subject of service-learning requirement since the idea was originally proposed. I no longer think it is unrelated to school; rather it is a very important educational experience."

3. "I have performed over 100 hours of community service in the past year....For the past year I have been serving two hours every other week at _____, a school for children who have no families or who have been neglected or abused. I go with other students from my youth group. We help the children with their homework, read to them, and play with them....

"I feel that interacting with people is a very good skill to learn, and community service has helped me with that. I'm not talking about stuffing envelopes, but doing the kind of service we do at _____. Those aren't skills that you're going to learn sitting in a classroom, and I think they are very important.

"Over the last three months I have also been helping to build a house for Habitat for Humanity....I go every Saturday with my mother for about four hours....I learned a lot of skills....almost all the people on the project are women. I think it's really nice working with a group of women, and showing men what we can do. It makes me feel very good that I can do it and it's a lot of fun working out there with my mother. Through this project I have also gained leadership skills. We work in small crews, and often I'm the one that's in charge because I'm there almost every week...."

4. "I believe that community service has gotten a pretty bad rap over the years....It is a good thing that it was required since I did some things that I may not have done if it was not needed for graduation. My main bulk of my community service was done at the Jerry Lewis Telethon. Wow. You want to talk about

overpowering....I was able to speak to a few people who had muscular dystrophy, and I had a great time with them. We palled around and answered phones and worked at one goal and one goal only, to get money and other types of donations to help people who were suffering from a disease that they had nothing to do with. When I was done, I felt good...."

5. "In this summer, I worked at Light House in _____ for community service. I had never worked before so this is my first experience. I was a little afraid of it but I thought that I need more experience which I had never experienced before. And my mother wanted me to do it because here is America. In Japan, Japanese won't do volunteers....People who work at Light House is very nice and kind. I can not speak English very well but they gave me enough job and teach me English ....Last thing, I have learned is to understand people who is rich or poor does not matter....I think I am little bit mature after this summer....I really thought America is great country."

6. "As this school year ends, I look back at the hours I spent serving the community at _____Elementary School. As a "helper in the media center, I helped the students both directly and indirectly....Instead of working so hard for themselves, all people should take time to help their community....People need to learn the wonderful satisfaction associated with helping others. Through my community service I learned how very important volunteers are to the world. I also learned how wonderful it is to serve society, and I encourage others to do the same."

7. "This summer I filled my community service requirement at the Jewish Community Center. I contributed my time to the day camp at the J.C.C. for second through fifth graders. My volunteer work consisted of being a co-counselor of fifteen third graders. This job was tough, but it also was a great deal of fun....Camp is definitely a great place to learn about responsibilities and to have fun at the same time. My community service was definitely educational, meaningful, and a sticky situation at some times. It is also something I will remember forever."

8. "I believe the way to true bliss and happiness is through helping our fellow man. I am achieving this through the community service program at _____ H.S....I did my volunteer work

at _____ Family Service. The slogan of this agency, "Care when you need it the most," caught my eye. Specifically I worked with children who from ages 8-12 were abused and neglected....

"In conclusion, the work and love I have given these children I hope will have at least a small effect on their lives. If they can at least remember the attention and fun I have given them, there is no more I can ask. I thank _____ H.S. for giving me the opportunity for the experience and the knowledge I have gained and shared and wish more students would look at community service as a blessing rather than a burden."

9. [Special education students and sophomore biology students worked together to build a children's garden featuring "a pond, tree house, gazebo, maze, topiaries, butterfly garden, and an array of perennials." The science students used their knowledge and skills from biology class to figure out the elements for an aquatic ecosystem for the garden. One female sophomore, interviewed for an article in the town's newspaper about the building of the pond, said:]

"When I'm done, I'll be proud because I can say I did it. So far I've got blisters, cut my knee, got a black and blue ankle. It's a lot of work."

The enthusiasm and support for community service that is expressed in such self-reflections are considerably stronger than the results of the survey data. Students recognized that what they learned through community service was significant to them. Community service was educational. Moreover, according to researchers on academic achievement in school such significant learning did not come at the expense of learning classroom knowledge.

Student Community Service Survey

Directions: Please complete this survey about your school's community service program. For questions 1-25 circle the appropriate number:

4 = strongly agree, 3 = somewhat agree, 2= somewhat disagree 1 = strongly disagree

1. My community service helps me to be aware of my responsibilities to my community.   4 3 2 1

2. My service activity helps me to expand my understanding of other people and their needs.   4 3 2 1

3. I believe that my service activity helps the community.   4 3 2 1

4. The service organization for which I work provided me with special training and/or safety training for that work.   4 3 2 1

5. My community service activity is more useful to me than an extra course in school would be (for example, a foundation course in English grammar).   4 3 2 1

6. I believe that community service is admirable and worthwhile.   4 3 2 1

7. I think that schools should require students to do community service.   4 3 2 1

8. My family supports my community service activity.   4 3 2 1

9. I discuss my service activity with my teachers in one or more of my classes.   4 3 2 1

10. My community service experience will change the way I think and act in the future as a citizen.   4 3 2 1

11. I think that my service activity creates a good will connection between my school and the community.   4 3 2 1

Figure 9. Survey tied to the three court cases administered to high school students in New Jersey.

12. I can and do use the knowledge and skills I learn
in my service activity (such as how to communicate
with other people) in other parts of my life.   4 3 2 1

13. I believe that I am learning to be a better problem
solver from service activity.   4 3 2 1

14. My service activity has developed and increased
my concern for my fellow human beings.   4 3 2 1

15. My service activity gives me a sense of confidence,
competence, and self-awareness.   4 3 2 1

16. My service activity gives me a sense of usefulness.   4 3 2 1

17. I believe that all people should participate in
community service in one manner or another.   4 3 2 1

18. My service activity promotes my being open-minded
about people and issues in our community.   4 3 2 1

19. I believe that my service activity helps me to
learn how to be a better citizen.   4 3 2 1

20. My service activity helps me to feel better about myself.   4 3 2 1

21. As a result of my service activity, I appreciate the
worth of community organizations more.   4 3 2 1

22. My service activity gives me the opportunity
to explore new roles and interests.   4 3 2 1

23. I believe that our school's community service
program helps to improve relations with the rest
of the community.   4 3 2 1

24. My service activity increases my ability to think
more clearly about people and community issues.   4 3 2 1

25. The service program I participate in has positive
effects for our community.   4 3 2 1

Figure 9. Survey tied to the three court cases administered to high school students in New Jersey.

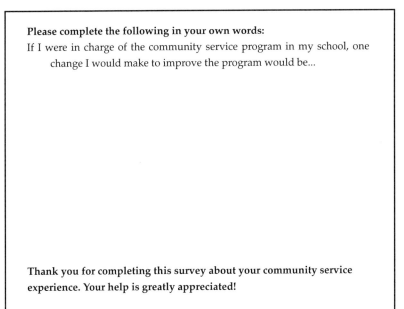

Please complete the following in your own words:
If I were in charge of the community service program in my school, one change I would make to improve the program would be...

Thank you for completing this survey about your community service experience. Your help is greatly appreciated!

Figure 9. Survey tied to the three court cases administered to high school students in New Jersey.

	Item #25	
	Disagree	Agree
Disagree	3 4%	2 3%
Agree	5 7%	61 86%

Item #6

Total = 71 students
100%

Item #6 = I believe that community service is admirable
and worthwhile. *(Steirer I at 1430).*

Item #25 = The service program I participate in has positive
effects for our community. *(Steirer I at 1339).*

Figure 10. Crosstabulation: "Admirable and Worthwhile" with "Positive
Effects of Service Activity"

Chapter VII: Remaining Issues and Concerns

Supervision and Liability

Students perform their community service outside of school except when they tutor other students in such subjects as mathematics, spelling, and reading, or prepare projects connected to out-of-school service. Thus, most of the time the school arranges with local outside organizations or individuals for the students to serve with them. Sometimes the organizations sign letters of cooperation and agree to supervise the students who serve through them. Whether an organization signs a letter of cooperation or not, the organization winds up supervising the students at its site.

Questions then arise. For example, to what extent is the supervising organization responsible for training the students to carry out their assigned tasks? To what extent is the supervising organization responsible for any injuries to the students? To what extent is the supervising organization liable for injuries that the students cause other people? To what extent and under what conditions is the student's school liable for injuries caused to others by the students? To what extent is the school liable for injuries to the students because it has not supervised and trained the students who are serving the community by mandate? To what extent are the students liable for injuries they cause to others?

Such supervision and liability questions did not arise in *Steirer*, *Immediato*, and *Herndon*. For this reason the legal relationships among students, school, and community agencies during times of mandatory community service are not yet clearly established by the courts. Nevertheless, the issue of supervision and liability is of concern to every high school community service program, especially mandatory ones in which students leave school to serve on sites where there is no direct supervision by school staff. School programs are subject to challenge by students, parents, and third parties in regard to the consequences of injuries to themselves and in regard to the costs of coping with liability for injuries (risk management and insurance).

Liability for injuries varies and depends generally on state law rather than federal law. Therefore, there is little to say here on a national level about liability. However, in recognition of the importance of community service to our federal government,

Congress enacted the Volunteer Protection Act of 1997 (Public Law 105-19; codified as 42 USC 14501). President Clinton signed the Act into law on June 18, 1997. In pertinent part the Volunteer Protection Act of 1997 states:

> "Sec.2 FINDINGS AND PURPOSE. (42 USC 14501)....
> (b)PURPOSE. The purpose of the Act is to promote the interests of social service program beneficiaries and taxpayers and to sustain the availability of programs, nonprofit organizations, and governmental entities that depend on volunteer contributions by reforming the laws to provide certain protections from liability abuses related to volunteers serving nonprofit organizations and governmental entities."

With the above purpose in mind, Congress set out to protect volunteers from "high liability costs and unwarranted litigation costs" (Findings, §2(a)(6)). As provided in the sections quoted below, volunteers are protected from liability, but service organizations are not. The Act also sets forth, among other key terms, a definition of a volunteer. Given that definition, does a student in a mandatory community service program qualify as a volunteer? In other words, of how much value is the half credit a student receives for community service? (Recall that without that half credit Steirer and Moralis did not receive their diplomas form Liberty High School in Bethlehem, Pennsylvania.)

> In pertinent part the Volunteer Protection Act of 1997 also provides:
> "SEC.4.LIMITATION ON LIABILITY FOR VOLUNTEERS (42 USC 14503)
> (a)LIABILITY PROTECTION FOR VOLUNTEERS. Except as provided in subsections (b) and (d), no volunteer of a nonprofit organization or governmental entity shall be liable for harm caused by an act or omission of the volunteer on behalf of the organization or entity if:
> (1)the volunteer was acting within the scope of the volunteer's responsibilities in the nonprofit organization or governmental entity at the time of the act or omission;

(2)if appropriate or required, the volunteer was properly licensed, certified, or authorized by the appropriate authorities for the activities or practice in the State in which the harm occurred, where the activities were or practice was undertaken within the scope of the volunteer's responsibilities in the non-profit organization or governmental entity;

(3)the harm was not caused by willful or criminal misconduct, gross negligence, reckless misconduct, or a conscious, flagrant indifference to the rights or safety of the individual harmed by the volunteer, and

(4)the harm was not caused by the volunteer operating a motor vehicle, vessel, aircraft, or other vehicle for which the State requires the operator or the owner of the vehicle, craft, or vessel to:

    (A)possess an operator's license: or

    (B)maintain insurance,

(b)CONCERNING RESPONSIBILITY OF VOLUNTEERS TO ORGANIZATIONS AND ENTITIES. Nothing in this section shall be construed to affect any civil action brought by any nonprofit organization or any governmental entity against any volunteer of such organization or entity.

(c)NO EFFECT ON LIABILITY OF ORGANIZATION OR ENTITY. Nothing in this section shall be construed to affect the liability of any nonprofit organization or governmental entity with respect to harm caused to any person....

Sec.6. DEFINITIONS. (42 USC 14505)

6)VOLUNTEER. The term "volunteer" means an individual performing services for a nonprofit organization or a governmental entity who does not receive:

(A)compensation (other than reasonable reimbursement or allowance for expenses actually incurred); or

(B)any other thing of value in lieu of compensation, in excess of $500 per year, and such term includes a volunteer serving as a director, officer, trustee, or direct service volunteer."

Risk Management

In light of the above key provisions, it is necessary for school leaders to confer with their individual attorneys and risk management advisors as to the impact of the entire Volunteer Protection Act of 1997 on their programs and students.

Even with volunteers being protected, the issues of liability and risk management, which includes insurance, are complex. Unfortunately, the literature dealing with liability and mandatory community service is almost non-existent in comparison with the literature on Fourteenth Amendment rights related to mandatory community service. In one of the few available pieces, Goldstein in his 1990 analysis of some of the issues begins by looking at injuries caused to others by volunteers during their service activity. He states, "Ordinarily the organization controlling the work site is responsible for acts of student interns, and injured parties would not, in most cases, be able to successfully sue the school or college."[365] He goes on to say that if, however, the injury to a third party was caused because "the student suffered from epilepsy and was prone to frequent lapses of consciousness, a fact known to school officials but not revealed by them to the agency," then "it is indeed possible that the school could be held responsible."[366] In short, the issue of liability is not simple.

If a student is injured while performing community service, the traditional assumption is that "a school has no liability for injuries which may occur when students are beyond the school's direct control."[367] Here, too, the issue is complex in that the key factors are the prior knowledge of the school and the actions taken by the school to assure that there are no unusual hazards connected with the service activity. Yet the situation presents a double bind. Goldstein puts it this way: "Administrators should be aware, however, that the more responsibility the school assumes for investigating the safety of activities, the more closely it may be held accountable. On the other hand, failure to aggressively determine if an activity is safe may itself make the school responsible."[368]

---

[365] Michael B. Goldstein, *Legal Issues in Combining Service and Learning, in Combining Service and Learning: A Resource Book for Community and Public Service,* Vol. II 39, 43 (J. C. Kendall and Associates eds., 1990).

[366] *Id.*

[367] *Id.* at 45.

[368] *Id.*

To minimize the liability, potential school leaders and the officials of the service organization need to engage in risk management. Hauge, an attorney who specializes in providing legal counseling for community-serving organizations, emphasizes the three tasks of a risk manager: to identify risks; to assess the potential liability from those risks; and to identify and implement methods of avoiding, controlling, or transferring the risks away from the organization.[369]

In performing those tasks the risk manager, in consultation with legal and insurance counselors, must constantly examine potential risks to clients, volunteers, and the organization. People involved in risk management must reject four common assumptions: that the organization (charitable or not) is immune from lawsuits; that because the organization has no knowledge about a volunteer's past conduct or conduct while performing service, the organization cannot be held liable for the volunteer's actions; that the public will forgive the organization just because it is charitable or a governmental agency and nonprofit; and that the organization's insurance will cover the liability.[370]

Schools have an obligation to their students who participate in community service. Typically these students report that they receive little or no safety or special training from the organizations they serve outside of school. Thus, leaders of community service programs need to seek counsel from professionals who know the local conditions regarding the relevant law and insurance requirements.

Just as there now is a federal law to protect volunteers so is there likely to be a state law to protect volunteers, nonprofit organizations, and/or charities. For example, in New Jersey the legislature in 1959 passed a Charitable Immunity Act (New Jersey Stat. Anno. 2A:53A-7). This Act, in pertinent part, provides as of its latest amendment in 1995:

2A:53A-7a. No nonprofit corporation, society, or association organized exclusively for religious, charitable, or educational purposes, or its trustees, directors, officers,

---

[369] J. C. Hauge presentation and paper at a conference on risk management for directors of volunteers of service organizations, "Volunteer Programs: A Risk Management Overview," Paramus, N.J., April 16, 1998.
[370] *Id.*

employees, agents, servants, or volunteers shall suffer damage from the negligence of any agent or servant of such corporation, society or association, where such person is a beneficiary, to whatever degree, of the works of such nonprofit corporation, society, or association....

Thus, in New Jersey a service student and a service organization will not be liable if injury results from negligence. However, the New Jersey Charitable Immunity Act goes on to exclude injuries due to intentional acts (in contrast to negligent acts), as well as to exclude injured people who are "unconcerned in and unrelated to and outside of the benefactions of such corporation, society, or association." The consequence of these provisions is that there exists only partial protection available by New Jersey statute.

School leaders in New Jersey and in other states with similar legislation will have to seek ways to manage the risks not protected by a combination of the federal Volunteer Protection Act of 1997 and their own state charitable immunity laws. Currently, the Bethlehem school district in its book that lists the many available approved service opportunities for its high school students now notes for each agency: Supervision provided by _____ "; "Training and/or Orientation"; whether the "agency carries liability insurance covering students on site"; whether the "agency participates in court ordered community service activities"; and "whether the agency requires Act 34 (criminal history)[371] clearance for employees." (As an example, see Figure 11, page 143.)

The supervision and liability issues for the schools remain significant despite the fact that the literature on community service for high school students typically does not cover the issues of supervision and liability and the court failed to take a position on supervision and liability issues.[372] In addition, risk management literature is typically addressed to the service organizations rather

---

[371] Act 34 of 1985 specifies that employees of public and private schools hired as of January 1, 1986 must undergo criminal record check by the Pennsylvania State Police. If a person stays within the same district, the background check is good indefinitely. Any break in service requires a new background check. The Pennsylvania State Police check "does not preclude the existence of criminal records which might be contained in the repositories of other local, state, or federal criminal justice agencies."

[372] The Steirer plaintiffs and lawyers at first considered using a claim based on lack of Act 34 compliance and notification. However, they decided not to do so in order to focus on constitutional issues. Telephone conversation with Eric Strauss, an attorney for the Steirer plaintiffs, Feb. 5, 1998.

than the schools.[373] The concern remains because of the money involved in liability matters, because of the potential personal pain and suffering that might result, and because of the negative impact any liability lawsuit might have on the future of a service program.

For these reasons school leaders need to consider risk management as an essential aspect of their efforts to provide a meaningful service program. A strategy to follow in this regard consists of five steps: "identify the risks; assess the risks; decide how to control the risks; implement a strategy to avoid, reduce, and deal with the risks; and review and revise periodically as needed."[374] A starting point in this regard is consideration of the key supervision and liability questions that appear below. "Risk management saves money, time, lives, and reputations....When it comes to liability risks, preparation is the key to prevention."[375]

Checklist of Key Supervision and Liability Questions

1. Is the service activity appropriate for the student's age and ability?
2. How does the service agency describe the activity and screen students for it?
3. Do the school and service agency have needed information about the student's health and medical conditions (e.g., allergies, disabilities) that might necessitate modification of the activity.
4. Does the service activity pose any safety risks to the student?
5. Have the student's parents given permission for this particular service activity?
6. Does the student in the service program understand his/her learning and service responsibilities?

---

[373] For example, the excellent book on the subject of risk management regarding service activities for students, *Kidding Around? Be Serious! A Commitment to Safe Service Opportunities for Young People* by Anna Seidman and John Patterson, is addressed to service organizations. The 1996 book is published by the Nonprofit Risk Management Center, located in Washington, D.C.

[374] *Id.* at 17.

[375] Hauge, *supra* 2.

7. Does the student understand what the school and service agency expect of him/her?
8. Does the school's insurance policy cover the student while serving in an off-campus site?
9. Does the service agency's insurance cover the student?
10. Who will supervise and who will train the student?
11. What supervision and training will the service agency provide?

Standards of Good Practice

Earlier, Chapter 2 presented a definition and purposes of community service. It did not, however, deal with what constitutes a good or excellent community service program. In *Steirer I* Judge Daniel H. Huyett noted that the original draft of the community service program for the Bethlehem Area School District possessed two components: (1)"classroom teaching and training of decision making, problem solving, and stress management skills"; and (2)the "required...actual service program."[376] The school district adopted only the second component. The judge noted that certain parts of the first component found their way into the second component upon adoption of the second part. He also noted that the adopted program did not require correlation of "a student's community service experience with that student's classroom coursework."[377] However, nowhere did he make any comment about the quality of the Bethlehem program with the absence of the essential aspects of the first component.

Was the draft program for Bethlehem a worthwhile program? Was it effective? Was it excellent? Was the program adopted worthwhile even though the board only adopted the second component? What constitutes a good or high quality community service program? That is, what are the standards of a high quality program? Is a community service program worthwhile even though it does not meet all the standards set forth for a high quality program? Should a board of education adopt a community service program even if it knows that the program does not meet all of the standards?

---

[376] Steirer I 789 F.Supp. at 1339.
[377] *Id.*

Two sets of standards, *The Principles of Good Practice for Combining Service and Learning* and *Standards of Quality for School-Based Service-Learning,* are available. Each was developed by a different group of people involved in community service. The two sets of standards explicitly refer to service and learning in their titles and in their content, distinguishing service-learning from the narrow definition of community service raised earlier in Chapter 2.[378] Both sets of standards also emphasize reflection as an essential element of a service program.

The Principles of Good Practice for Combining Service and Learning[379]

The 10 principles that follow derive from consultation with more than 70 groups involved in service and learning and conducted by the National Society for Experiential Education. The preamble to and the language of The Principles of Good Practice that follow are the work of an advisory group which met in May, 1989. The Preamble and the 10 Principles are:

> We are a nation founded upon active citizenship and participation in community life. We have always believed that individuals can and should serve. It is crucial that service toward the common good be combined with reflective learning to assure that service programs of high quality can be created and sustained over time, and to help individuals appreciate how service can be a significant and ongoing part of life. Service, combined with learning, adds value to each and transforms both.

---

[378] The following statement appears regarding the distinction: "Although the terms are sometimes used interchangeably, service-learning and community service are not synonymous. Community service may be, and often is, a powerful experience for young people, but community service becomes service-learning when there is deliberate connection made between service and learning opportunities which are then accompanied by conscious and thoughtfully-designed occasions for reflecting on their service experience." Alliance for Service Learning in Education Reform, *Standards of Quality for School-Based Service Learning* 5 (May 1993).

[379] E. P. Honnet and S. J. Poulsen, *Principles of Good Practice for Combining Service and Learning: A Wingspread Report* 1-2 (October 1989).

Those who serve and those who are served are thus able to develop the informed judgment, imagination, and skills that lead to a greater capacity to contribute to the common good.

The Principles that follow are a statement of what we believe are essential components of good practice. We invite you to use them in the context of your particular needs and purposes.

1. An effective program engages people in responsible and challenging actions for the common good.

2. An effective program provides structured opportunities for people to reflect critically on their service experience.

3. An effective program articulates clear service and learning goals for everyone involved.

4. An effective program allows for those with needs to define those needs.

5. An effective program clarifies the responsibilities of each person and organization involved.

6. An effective program matches service providers and service needs through a process that recognizes changing circumstances.

7. An effective program expects genuine, active, and sustained organizational commitment.

8. An effective program includes training, supervision, monitoring, support, recognition, and evaluation to meet service and learning goals.

9. An effective program insures that the time commitment for service and learning is flexible, appropriate, and in the best interests of all involved.

10. An effective program is committed to program participation by and with diverse populations.[380]

---

[380] *Id.* at 1-2.

Standards of Quality for School-Based Service-Learning[381]

The Standards of Quality for School-based Service-learning are the work of the eight-member Standards Committee of the Alliance for Service-Learning in Education Reform. In introducing the Standards of Quality, the Standards Committee recognized that it was not providing "a list of absolutes, nor even a complete inventory of the elements that contribute to high quality. Instead, what follows is designed to serve as a yardstick that can be used to measure the success of a variety of approaches to service-learning, locally as well as nationally."[382] The Standards Committee went on to state that the "model should be modified to reflect the maturity and capacities of youth at different stages. Duration of the service role, type of service, desired outcomes, and the structure for reflection must be designed to be age-appropriate."[383]

The 11 Standards of Quality are:

1. Effective service-learning efforts strengthen service and academic learning.
2. Model service-learning provides concrete opportunities for youth to learn new skills, to think critically, and to test new roles in an environment which encourages risk-taking and rewards competence.
3. Preparation and reflection are essential elements in service-learning.
4. Students' efforts are recognized by their peers and the community they serve.
5. Youth are involved in the planning.
6. The service students perform makes a meaningful contribution to the community.
7. Effective service-learning integrates systematic formative and summative evaluation.
8. Service-learning connects school and its community in new and positive ways.
9. Service-learning is understood and supported as an integral element in the life of a school and its community.
10. Skilled adult guidance and supervision is essential to the success of service-learning.

---

[381] Alliance for Service-Learning in Education Reform, *Standards of Quality for School-Based Service Learning* 3-5 (May 1993).
[382] *Id.* at 4.
[383] *Id.* at 5.

11. Pre-service and staff development which includes the philosophy and methodology of service-learning best ensure that program quality and continuity are maintained.[384]

Community Service Activities Guidelines

Phyllis Walsh, the founder and current coordinator of community service for the Bethlehem Area School District, offers a set of Community Service Activities Guidelines. These Guidelines reflect the Bethlehem program that is explicitly a community service program in the narrow meaning of that term. Walsh recognizes this difference in that the Bethlehem high schools currently also offer service-learning opportunities for certain classroom groups. She does not speak in terms of principles or standards but of goals. Also, she avoids the terms service-learning and reflection, two fundamental terms in the above two sets of standards.[385]

According to Walsh, community service activities: should be ones designed to actively engage students in tasks. Community Service should also meet the following goals:

1. Be developmentally appropriate and supervised by a responsible adult;

2. Provide needed services to the community or to the service agency's clientele;

3. Provide tangible benefits rather than being limited to housekeeping duties or chores;

4. Promote healthy psychological, intellectual, and social development, including self-esteem and self-actualization;

5. Promote career exploration and work force skills;

6. Emphasize benefits to both youth and society; and

7. Emphasize assumption of the responsibilities and obligations of life as well as the enjoyment of its privileges.

Service activities should not do the following:

---

[384] *Id.* at 3.
[385] Recall the reference to the Bethlehem community service program in Steirer I, 789 F.Supp. at 1339; and in Steirer II, 987 F.2d at 992.

1. Pose unusual safety risks;
2. Involve operation of motor vehicles or use of machinery that requires technical training;
3. Displace paid employees;
4. Provide private or personal financial gain;
5. Promote doctrinal or religious issues; or
6. Be illegally discriminatory in regard to age, sex, religion, or race.[386]

Integrating Community Service with Academic Content

The Standards Committee of the Alliance for Service-Learning, unlike the Advisory Group for the Principles of Good Practice and Phyllis Walsh, does explicitly advocate the integration of community service with the ongoing, regular academic curriculum. In commenting about service-learning efforts in the clarification of its very first standard the Standards Committee wrote, "The examples that follow demonstrate that service can be linked to academics in many ways, and at all levels."[387] The Committee then gave an example of tying service with the classroom curriculum: "In secondary school, adolescents can explore issues such as hunger through virtually every academic discipline: crop rotation and rainfall in science and geography, computing individual and collective nutritional needs in math class, the economics of food distribution and efforts of governments to address these problems in social studies, and so on. Service at a food distribution center could reinforce all this learning by placing it in the context of community needs."[388]

In this way the Standards Committee goes much further with its "service-learning" position than the Advisory Group's service and learning Principles and Walsh's Community Service Activities Guidelines, which do not mention learning. The Standards

---

[386] Phyliss V. Walsh, *Service Learning, in Educational Innovation: An Agenda to Frame the Future* 93, 107, (C. E. Greenawalt, II ed., 1994).
[387] Alliance for Service Learning, at 6.
[388] *Id.*

Committee wants an explicit and direct "link" of service with learning in the overall academic dimension of the school. Such a link is much more than a short term effort by a guidance counselor working in a career exploration course or unit (as in the Rye Neck High School community service program[389]) and much more than having a service organization's staff members talk briefly with students about their service activities. In sum, service is to be infused into the school's curriculum so that it becomes one with learning; it becomes service-learning.

The Compatibility of Service-Learning and Academic Content Standards

To show how community service can be so linked, or integrated, at least in New Jersey, John Battaglia, for 19 years the first and only coordinator of community service at Fort Lee High School (Fort Lee, New Jersey), prepared a grid related to the New Jersey Core Curriculum Content Standards which were adopted in 1996.[390] (See Figure 12, pages 144-151.)

The New Jersey core curriculum content standards, prepared by the state's Department of Education "are an attempt to define the meaning of Thorough in the context of the 1875 State constitutional guarantee that students would be educated within a Thorough and Efficient system of free public schools [Article VIII, Section 4, Paragraph 1 of the current 1947 revised New Jersey Constitution]."[391]

The content standards are not intended to be a curriculum guide but a definition of expected results. The emphasis on cross-content workplace readiness standards appears through five

---

[389] *See* Immediato I, 873 F. Supp. 846 *and* Immediato II, 73 F.3d 454.

[390] Battaglia had testified previously in 1995 when the Core Curriculum Content Standards were still being considered that "the New Jersey State Department of Education recognize the importance of service-learning as a viable and essential element of a thorough and efficient education for youth and that every school district in the state develop a plan for youth service which adequately reflects the needs and the priorities of that community." J. Battaglia, "Testimony Presented to the Representatives of the New Jersey State Department of Education on the Question of a Thorough and Efficient Education" 1, Paramus, N.J. (Sept. 14, 1995).

[391] New Jersey State Department of Education, *Core Curriculum Content Standards* (May 1996).

standards that relate to seven academic core curriculum content areas. The five workplace readiness standards are:

1. All students will develop career planning and workplace readiness skills.
2. All students will use technology, information, and other tools.
3. All students will use critical thinking, decision-making, and problem-solving skills.
4. All students will demonstrate self-management skills.
5. All students will apply safety principles.[392]

The seven academic core curriculum content areas listed alphabetically are:
1. Visual and Performing Arts
2. Comprehensive Health and Physical Education
3. Language Arts/Literacy
4. Mathematics
5. Science
6. Social Studies
7. World Languages[393]

The seven content areas have a combined total of 56 standards, with each standard clarified and specified further by Cumulative Progress Indicators. The many indicators are divided into three parts to show "what students need to know and be able to do by the end of grades 4, 8, and 11-12."[394] (These are the grade levels at which state testing occurs in New Jersey.) The workplace readiness standards also have many Cumulative Progress Indicators.

In Figure 14, Battaglia cross-hatched the five workplace readiness standards against selected cumulative progress indicators from each of the seven content areas. He listed the selected progress indicators and gave each its classification numbers (i.e., content area, standard, and progress indicator). He then offered a Service Application (S.A.) to show how and what teachers and students might do to "interconnect" service-learning with the core curriculum content standards. The Service Application appears in bold print in Battaglia's chart. In this way Battaglia has offered a host of specific examples of the kind of linking/integrating hinted at

---

[392] *Id.* at ii.
[393] *Id.* at iii.
[394] *Id.* at vii.

by the Standards Committee of the Alliance for Service. Battaglia's chart will be informative and helpful to understand what some educators advocate for community service in the public schools. The Service Applications offered by the chart concretize the Principles, Standards, and Guidlines offered earlier as approaches for determining what good practice is regarding community service.

The Cecil County (Maryland) Approach to Its State's Community Service Requirement

On July 29,1992, the Maryland State Board of Education passed a requirement, beginning with the Class of 1997, of performance of community service for graduation from high school. The new law, part of the General Instructional Programs section of the Code of Maryland Regulations, is:

D. Student Service. Students shall complete one of the following:
(1) 75 hours of student service that includes preparation, action, and reflection components and that, at the discretion of the local school system, may begin during the middle grades; or
(2) A locally designed program in student service that has been approved by the State Superintendent of Schools. (Code of Maryland Regulations, Department of Education, Title 13A:03.02.03).

At first, the Cecil County Board of Education prepared its own 75-hour program. However, after three years of experience with the "clock-hours" approach, Cecil County revised its program for several reasons, most importantly the realization that community service was more meaningful to students when tied closely to the classroom curriculum. The revision also yielded the avoidance of keeping track of students in order to be sure of regarding the timely completion of their hours of service.

In August 1996 the Cecil County Public School began a transition to its revised approach: students now fulfill Maryland's mandatory community service requirement by performing service integrated with four service-learning projects in Grades 6, 7, 8, and 9. "These projects are multi-disciplinary units which facilitate the subject area curriculum."[395]   The four Service-Learning Projects are:

> 6th grade — The Environment and You
> 7th grade — Food for Thought
> 8th grade — Saving the Past for the Future
> 9th grade — Issues in Our Society

Each Service-Learning Project appears in its own book with specific guidelines for the teacher, focusing on the three phases of Preparation, Action, and Reflection that are mentioned in the law. The sixth grade project is "very teacher directed," the seventh and eighth-grade projects give students "more responsibility," and the ninth-grade project "is essentially student-directed."[396]

In addition to gaining the advantages claimed for integrating community service with the classroom curriculum as well as avoiding the aggravations associated with the clock-hours approach to community service, Cecil County has lowered the age at which its students may begin to fulfill the community service requirement. It has found that middle school teachers and the middle school curriculum are more flexible in their approaches to community service than high school teachers who are often resistant to changes in the curriculum and fearful of not "covering" their specified subject matter.

As a result, Cecil County is pleased with its revised service-learning program whose goal is "to empower students to improve their communities as well as their own problem solving and interpersonal skills."[397]   Teachers receive more staff development training, especially for integrating the learning projects into their regular classroom curriculum and for learning techniques to guide the critical reflection of students on their service experiences. Students who complete additional, approved service projects outside of school will earn Meritorious Service-Learning Hours that will be listed on their portfolios, high school report cards, and academic transcripts. The county and state will recognize students who design high quality projects.[398]

---

[395] Cecil County Public Schools (Elkton, Maryland), *Saving the Past for the Future: Service Learning Unit*, Grade 8, 8 (March, 1997).

[396] *Id.*

[397] *Id.* My visit to the schools in Elkton, Maryland, and my interviews with the staff and students there corroborate the literature published by the school district.

[398] *Id.*

Conclusion

It is appropriate at this point to present what are considered the results of effective, good practice. The following short summary, written as part of the report containing the Principles of Good Practice for Combining Service and Learning, will offer another insight into the perspective of that report's Advisory Group and serve as a supplement to the review of the outcomes of community service presented in Chapter 6.

The advisory group wrote:

> The combination of service and learning is powerful. It creates potential benefits beyond what either service or learning can offer separately. The frequent results of the effective interplay of service and learning are that participants:
> • Develop a habit of critical reflection on their experiences, enabling them to learn more throughout life,
> • Are more curious and motivated to learn,
> • Are able to perform better service,
> • Strengthen their ethic of social and civic response,
> • Feel more committed to addressing the underlying problems behind social issues,
> • Understand problems in a more complex way and can imagine alternative solutions,
> • Demonstrate more sensitivity to how decisions are made and how institutional decisions affect people's lives,
> • Learn how to work more collaboratively with other people on real problems,
> • Realize that their lives can make a difference."[399]

Future legal challenges may well involve the standards of good practice and the research on outcomes of community service to a greater extent than seen in the previous lawsuits.

---

[399] Honnet and Poulsen, *supra,* at 2-3.

Name of Agency/Organization: Bethlehem Area
School District — Lincoln Elementary School
Address: 1810 Renwick Street, Bethlehem, PA 18017-6199
Phone number: 866-8722 **Contact Person:** Peggy Capozzolo

****

Number of students requested: unlimited   **Minimum age:** 13
Description of service opportunities: Tutoring for students in grades 1-5
Minimum Time of Service Per Shift or Session: 45 minutes
Hours agency is open to community service students:
Monday-Friday, 2:30 p.m. - 3:15 p.m.

****

Dress requirements: school attire
Supervision provided by: School district employees
Training and/or orientation: Will be scheduled as needed.

****

Additional information/comments:

Map Reference: Map D, Site 11

This agency carries liability insurance covering students	(Yes)
This agency participates in court order community service activities	(No)
This agency requires Act 34 (criminal history) clearance for employees	(Yes)

Figure 11. Listing of Community Service Opportunity

Figure 12. Core Curriculum Content Standards as Related to Workplace Readiness Skills and Service-Learning. Prepared by John Battaglia.

The intent of this chart is to demonstrate the compatibility of service-learning, the cross-content workplace readiness standards, and the core curriculum standards for seven academic areas. The chart provides only a limited glimpse of the infinite interconnections of service-learning with the cumulative progress indicators for the core curriculum content standards.

CROSS-CONTENT WORKPLACE READINESS STANDARDS WITH SERVICE APPLICATION (S.A.)

A. DEVELOP CAREER PLANNING AND WORK PLACE READINESS SKILLS

1. Visual and performing Arts

Demonstrate knowledge of how artists and artistic works connect with political, social and cultural, and historic events. 1.5.8. **S.A.: Serve as guide and docent at local or regional arts centers and museums.**

2. Comprehensive Health and Physical Education

Identify and demonstrate health practices that support and enhance personal and family physical and mental health. 2.1.10. **S.A.: High school peer facilitators instruct middle and elementary school children while exploring a possible career choice; candy stripers serve at local hospitals.**

3. Language Arts/ Literacy

Speak before a group to express thoughts and ideas, convey opinion, present information, and tell a story. 3.1.8. **S.A.: 4th grade student volunteers perform skits for 1st and 2nd graders about people in their community (e.g. firemen, police, teachers) and their occupations.**

4. Mathematics

Recognize, formulate, and solve problems arising from mathematical situations, everyday experiences, applications to other disciplines and career applications, 4.1.16. **S.A.: Student volunteers at Habitat for Humanity use math skills and formulas to implement proper construction applications.**

5. Science

Explain how organisms are affected by different components of an ecosystem and the flow of energy through it. 5.6.11. **S.A.: Student volunteers at a local environmental center explore a possible career as a naturalist while they serve as guides and instructors on the local ecosystem to visitors and to younger children.**

6. Social Science	Analyze the functioning of the executive, judicial, and legislative branches of government. 6.1.8. **S.A.: With an eye toward possible future public service, student volunteers intern within the office of a local or state legislator or with a county prosecutor, study the relationship between the branches of government.**
7. World Languages	Respond to and initiate simple statements and commands such as greetings, introductions, and leave-taking. 7.1.1. **S.A.: An elementary school volunteer "greeter club" greets new students, indicates in a foreign language the important areas within the school, and asks new students about life and jobs in their native countries.**

CROSS-CONTENT WORKPLACE READINESS STANDARDS WITH SERVICE APPLICATION (S.A.)

B. USER TECHNOLOGY, INFORMATION, AND OTHER TOOLS

1. Visual and Performing Arts	Demonstrate an understanding of technology, methods, materials, and creative processes commonly used in dance, music, theater, or visual arts. 1.3.3. **S.A.: Student use of computers, advanced musical instrumentality, and dedicated lighting systems to serve in schools, community theaters, recreation departments, and community-based organizations.**
2. Comprehensive Health and Physical Education	Describe a healthy adult, discuss physical and mental health problems, and use health assessment data to develop strategies for reducing health problems and related risk factors. 2.1.15. **S.A.: Student volunteers (for the American Heart Association or the local mental health center) use computer technology and standardized tests to develop and assess data regarding adolescent eating and drinking habits. Data are used to inform students of positive ways to change harmful behavior.**
3. Language Arts/ Literacy	Gather and synthesize data for research from a variety of sources, including print materials, technological resources, observations, interviews, and audiovisual media. 3.4.25. **S.A.: Environmental student volunteers gather research information on local waterways and air pollution using computer data and barometric equipment for assessment, all of which will result in a written service action plan.**

Figure 12. Core Curriculum Content Standards as Related to Workplace Readiness Skills and Service-Learning. Prepared by John Battaglia.

The intent of this chart is to demonstrate the compatibility of service-learning, the cross-content work-place readiness standards, and the core curriculum standards for seven academic areas. The chart provides only a limited glimpse of the infinite interconnections of service-learning with the cumulative progress indicators for the core curriculum content standards.

CROSS-CONTENT WORKPLACE READINESS STANDARDS WITH SERVICE APPLICATION (S.A.)

B. USER TECHNOLOGY, INFORMATION, AND OTHER TOOLS

4. Mathematics	Use calculators and computers effectively and efficiently in applying mathematical concepts and principles to various types of problems. 4.5.8. **S.A.: High school math tutors use age-appropriate computer games and software such as "Math Blaster" in the tutorial of elementary school children.**
5. Science	Use computer spread sheets, graphing, and database programs to assist in quantitative analysis. 5.5.12. **S.A.: Calculus volunteers tutor their peers in the use and applications of computers, spreadsheets, and other programs that are part of their school curriculum.**
6. Social Studies	Analyze the impact of human migration on physical and human systems. 6.8.13. **S.A.: Student volunteers to local municipalities use computers and graphs to analyze local migration trends in order to understand the demands on and needs for basic services, such as education, recreation, and emergency services.**
7. World Languages	Use technology to enhance language acquisition and to acquire current cultural information in order to develop more accurate impressions of the culture studies. 7.2.13. **S.A.: High school "language bank" volunteers use the computer and their study of a foreign language and culture to translate signs and other information for the schools, the municipality, and local businesses.**

CROSS-CONTENT WORKPLACE READINESS STANDARDS WITH SERVICE APPLICATION (S.A.)

C. USE CRITICAL-THINKING, DECISION-MAKING, AND PROBLEM-SOLVING SKILLS

1. Visual and Performing Arts	Identify and solve design problems in space, structures, objects, sound, and/or events for home and workplace. 1.6.3. S.A.: **Students plan, design, and implement indoor and outdoor recreational space which would be ecologically and aesthetically safe and pleasing.**
2. Comprehensive Health and Physical Education	Analyze the causes of conflict and violent behavior in youth and adults and describe non-violent strategies for individuals and groups to prevent and solve conflict. 2.2.10. **S.A.: Peer and cross-age student mediators analyze negative student behavior and develop games and "trust" exercises which focus on cooperative and positive group effort.**
3. Language Arts/Literacy	Begin to identify common aspects of human existence. 3.4.18. S.A.: Student volunteers analyze the causes and effects of hunger and poverty in today's society with an eye toward developing specific service projects which address these concerns locally.
4. Mathematics authentic	Determine, collect, organize, and analyze data needed to solve problems. 4.1.8. **S.A.: Student volunteers at the local Historic Park gather and analyze data which describe the proper weights and sizes of stones needed for the reconstruction of revolutionary period walls and ramparts in preparation for the building of these structures.**
5. Science	Communicate experimental findings using words, charts, pictures, and diagrams. 5.2.9. **S.A.: Student volunteers analyze data regarding the basic community services of water drainage and sewerage removal as a way to improve same. Findings are reported to the appropriate borough officials in the form of charts, graphs, and diagrams.**
6. Social Studies	Understand the views of people of other times and places regarding the issues they have faced. 6.3.12. **S.A.: Nursing home volunteers interview senior citizens to learn about recent past history while making "friendly visitations." Students analyze the past while comparing and contrasting those trends with current geo-political events with an eye towards improving conditions through student service.**
7. World Languages	Identify some common distinct features, such as parts of speech and vocabulary, among languages. 7.1.7. **S.A.: Student linguistic volunteers develop an information booklet in one or more foreign languages as an aide to foreign born perspective volunteers in hospitals and other human service agencies.**

Figure 12. Core Curriculum Content Standards as Related to Workplace Readiness Skills and Service-Learning. Prepared by John Battaglia

The intent of this chart is to demonstrate the compatibility of service-learning, the cross-content workplace readiness standards, and the core curriculum standards for seven academic areas. The chart provides only a limited glimpse of the infinite interconnections of service-learning with the cumulative progress indicators for the core curriculum content standards.

CROSS-CONTENT WORKPLACE READINESS STANDARDS WITH SERVICE APPLICATION (S.A.)

D. DEMONSTRATE SELF-MANAGEMENT SKILLS

1. Visual and Performing Arts	Create works of art that communicate personal opinions, thoughts, and ideas. 1.5.10. S.A.: **Create and donate pieces of art to hospitals, nursing homes, and nonprofit agencies, and describe to the recipients the motive and concept which lead to their creation.**
2. Comprehensive Health and Physical Education	Describe the characteristics of skilled performance in a variety of physical activities. 2.5.7. S.A.: **Student volunteers in recreation departments and organized sport teams instruct youth regarding the safe and proper techniques of skilled performances.**
3. Language Arts/ Literacy	Read and use printed materials and technical manuals from other disciplines, such as science, social studies, mathematics, and applied technology. 3.4.16. S.A.: **8th grade students use appropriate botanical and horticultural manuals and make any necessary site adjustments in order to implement a school vegetable and flower garden as part of a group service project.**

4. Mathematics	Recognize that there may be multiple ways to solve a problem, weigh their relative merits, and select and use appropriate problem-solving strategies. 4.1.13. **S.A.: Volunteers in a recreation department's aerobics program develop appropriate exercise regimens for different children to maximize exercise, caloric reduction, and exercise time.**
5. Science	Monitor local weather conditions and changes in the atmosphere that lead to weather systems. 5.10.9. **S.A.: Student municipal volunteers monitor local weather conditions and seasonal fluctuations in temperatures and rainfall in an attempt to catalog optimal times and to make adjustments for public water usage, planting of municipal plants and shrubs, and outdoor recreation events.**
6. Social Studies	Identify rights and responsibilities of citizens. 6.1.2. **S.A.: Student volunteers recognize and choose a local human need such as "homelessness" and serve in agencies that address the problem.**
7. World Languages	Communicate and interact in a limited range of task-oriented and social situations. 7.1.17. **S.A.: High school service volunteers and foreign language students use their linguistic skills to visit ESL and bilingual classes in order to describe volunteer opportunities for students with little or no understanding of English.**

CROSS-CONTENT WORKPLACE READINESS STANDARDS WITH SERVICE APPLICATION (S.A.)

E. APPLY SAFETY PRINCIPLES

1. Visual and Performing Arts	Plan and execute solutions to design problems. 1.6.2. **S.A.: Elementary students design and implement a flower and vegetable garden to meet community needs (donations to nursing homes and welfare recipients); they learn about the proper use of garden tools and to work safely in groups to develop their service projects.**
2. Comprehensive Health and Physical Education	Describe and demonstrate the application of appropriate rules, strategies, and sportsmanship behaviors as a participant in and as an observer of physical activities. 2.5.9. **S.A.: High school student athletes serve as coaches and instructors to younger children.**

Figure 12. Core Curriculum Content Standards as Related to Workplace Readiness Skills and Service-Learning. Prepared by John Battaglia

The intent of this chart is to demonstrate the compatibility of service-learning, the cross-content workplace readiness standards, and the core curriculum standards for seven academic areas. The chart provides only a limited glimpse of the infinite interconnections of service-learning with the cumulative progress indicators for the core curriculum content standards.

CROSS-CONTENT WORKPLACE READINESS STANDARDS WITH SERVICE APPLICATION (S.A.)

E. APPLY SAFETY PRINCIPLES

3. Language Arts/ Literacy	Write technical materials, such as instructions for playing a game, that include specific details 3.3.16. **S.A.: 8th grade service volunteers will write safety rules and procedures for younger children to follow while engaging in outdoor group activities such as "duck duck goose" and "hide and seek."**
4. Mathematics	Generate, collect, organize, and represent these data in tables, charts, and graphs. 4.12.9. **S.A.: Student volunteers to the community collect appropriate data on traffic flow and density in order to improve local traffic safety and rush hour flow through town.**
5. Science	Identify and explain factors that influence water quality needed to sustain life. 5.10.14. **S.A.: Within a "water watch" like service project, student volunteers apply appropriate safety principles and techniques to monitor water quality and to clean-up streams and ponds.**

6. Social Studies	Use and interpret maps and other graphical representations to analyze, explain, and solve geographical problems. 6.7.11. S.A.: **Student volunteer interns within the county urban planning department utilize appropriate safety and road awareness principles as they interpret relief maps and traverse local roadways in an attempt to collect data and analyze information concerning changes in mass transit options.**
7. Word Languages	Use technology to enhance language acquisitions and to acquire cultural information in order to develop more accurate impressions of the culture studies. 7.2.13. S.A.: **While interviewing native speakers in their communities, foreign language students use a tape recorder and a computer to record, practice, and analyze legitimate and slang words and phrases. Students apply all appropriate safety principles and consideration in data gathering outside the schools and in conjunction with local customs and circumstances.**

Chapter VIII: Final Comments

The unanimous victories in court by the defendant boards of education in Bethlehem, Pennsylvania, Rye Neck, New York, and Chapel Hill, North Carolina are significant in respect to curricular and governmental reasons. In regard to the curriculum, the victories signal the legitimacy of connecting traditional in-class academic course content with experiential out-of-class service activity. The federal courts accepted the reasoning offered by the defendant school districts for believing that mandatory community service is beneficial educationally to participating students. After stating the purposes and some outcomes of community service, Judge Bullock in *Herndon I* said, "The Chapel Hill-Carrboro Board of Education could reasonably conclude that the Program is rationally related to the legitimate state interest of educating students enrolled in its public schools and in preparing them for participation in society as citizens."[400]

The victories are also significant in that the courts have supported local boards of education in their efforts to determine what is good educational policy for their students. The courts have not attempted to override locally established and approved bodies. They have recognized that boards of education, not the courts, have the responsibility to establish policy for their communities. They have not permitted a small number of plaintiffs to create a situation in which the authority of a local board is weakened under the claim that a policy decision was "arbitrary and irrational."[401] In this way not only did mandatory community service programs win but local governmental bodies won renewed strength as policy makers for their communities.

Moreover, the courts sustained the legal acceptability of mandatory community service programs without requiring that they meet any standards of good practice (at least partly because the plaintiffs never brought suit against the substance of the programs but only against the requirement of the program). Also, the courts did not demand research results from the defendants to demonstrate that their programs were achieving the established purposes set for community service. The courts felt no great need to demand research results because the plaintiffs never complained

---

[400] Herndon I, 899 F.Supp. at 1453.
[401] *Id.*

about the value and outcomes of community service and because the courts had accepted the rational basis, a low standard, as its appropriate legal standard for reviewing the decision of another governmental agency.

In regard to not reviewing outcome data to support the claims that community service is beneficial to students, the courts were discreet in their decisions. The research data from surveys and other quantitative methods are not conclusive that community service experience increases student academic learning or civic participation. The quantitative data on learning, as reported earlier,[402] only show that community service does not detract from academic learning. The strongest data support the psychological and social development purpose. Conrad, a researcher and reviewer of the available research, has stated, "In fact, the most consistent finding of studies of participatory programs is that these experiences do tend to increase self-esteem and promote personal development."[403]

The courts had access to affidavits and reports about the efficacy of community service from experienced educators and participating students. In addition, there is no rule anywhere that survey and other quantitative data outweigh personal data and are needed to justify a board of education's decision. Such quantitative data also do not often exist to support other graduation requirements so as to make policy-making criteria consistent. The result is that the courts' approaches to their reviews further legitimated the existing data and the personal testimony of educators and students. In sum, data on the psychological and social development purpose and student personal accounts that praised community service appeared to have been sufficient for the courts to support reasonable board of education decisions.

The victories of the defendants are also significant regarding the state's interest in the education of children. While the courts have agreed that parents may direct the education of their children, they recently have stated repeatedly that the rights of parents are limited once the parents decide to enroll their children in public schools. The courts have refused to allow parents to opt-out selectively from requirements set by authorized boards of education, either elected boards or boards appointed by elected officials.

---

[402] See the second part of Chapter 6.
[403] Dan Conrad, School-Community Participation for Social Studies, in *Handbook on Research on Social Studies Teaching and Learning*, 540, 543 (J. P. Shaver ed., 1991).

The Supreme Court, for whatever reason, has refused to grant petitions requesting reviews of decisions dealing with parental rights as non-fundamental ones. It is in recognition of this fact that the proposed and successful legislation explicitly refers to parental rights as fundamental rights with the expectation that courts will utilize a high standard when reviewing them. In any case, the legitimacy of the state's interest in every child's education was renewed with emphasis in each of the three court cases.

In sum, with these victories the courts have supported community service and the role of local boards of education in deciding policy issues within their discretion. The plaintiffs, too, it must be remembered, also supported the value of community service for both the student and the community. The plaintiffs did not object to the substance of the service programs, only to the requirement of it for graduation. As Judge Sloviter noted, "Although both minor plaintiffs [Lynn Ann Steirer and David Stephen Moralis] have performed and intend to continue performing volunteer work on their own time, they object to being forced to engage in community service as a graduation requirement."[404] This acceptance of the value of service shows the success of educators who have advocated for the inclusion of experiential civic education into the traditionally classroom-bound high school curriculum. Given the number of students covered by mandatory requirements, the low number of lawsuits and the now quiet court scene are testimony to the acceptance of community service as a legitimate part of a high school's curriculum. It is helpful to keep in mind that only five students and their parents have appeared in court up until now.

In light of these legal, educational, and governmental victories it is surprising that not more boards of education support a broader-based community service program, either mandatory or voluntary. The benefits to students in regard to personal development, academic development, and civic education as well as the goodwill engendered by closer ties between the schools and their communities certainly appear to be compelling, especially now that the threat of costly legal action appears to be removed. The financing of a community service program appears to be quite low in relation to the expected benefits. As Battaglia stated in his testimony before the New Jersey Department of Education, "To conclude, I submit that youth service and service-learning works.

---

[404] Steirer II, 987 F.2d at 992.

It can be implemented with no additional money in the case of co-curricular options or for little money, depending on a district's needs and priorities."[405] Many varieties are possible in voluntary programs, as shown by the current approach adopted by the Cecil County (Maryland) Public Schools.[406]

Despite the three significant victories for mandatory community service the future is not perfectly clear. Future legal challenges are still possible but are not likely to repeat the five federal constitutional claims already brought by plaintiffs. Instead, legal challenges will likely arise out of injuries to or by students involved in community service or be based on new state constitutional amendments or state statutes. (At this point no proposed federal statute that will be helpful to prospective plaintiffs is on the horizon.) The precise shape of such lawsuits and their future effects on service programs nationwide are not discernible at this time.

Mandatory community service appears to have survived an initial attack in the courts, in Congress, in state legislatures, and in the voting booths at the local firehouses. It appears that the public favors community service by young people in some form or another and derives satisfaction from knowing that American youth is learning to take its place as participating members of society. At this point, having won the support of the courts, community service programs in American high schools most likely will continue to survive and probably will prosper if the participants' self-reflections presented in this book and elsewhere have any influence on local boards of education.

---

[405] Battaglia, *supra* at 2.
[406] See the last section of Chapter 7.

Table of Cases

Table of Figures